A CANADIAN SATURDAY NIGHT

GREY*S*TONE BOOKS
Douglas & McIntyre Publishing Group
Vancouver/Toronto/Berkeley

"I WOULD RATHER HAVE PLAYED FOR THE LEAFS THAN BE PRIME MINISTER OF CANADA."

Lester B. Pearson, prime minister of Canada, 1963–1968

Greystone Books
A division of Douglas & McIntyre Ltd.
2323 Quebec Street, Suite 201
Vancouver, British Columbia
Canada V5T 4S7
www.greystonebooks.com

Library and Archives Canada Cataloguing in Publication
Podnieks, Andrew
A Canadian saturday night : hockey and the culture of a country /
Andrew Podnieks.
ISBN-13: 978-1-55365-201-4 · ISBN-10: 1-55365-201-0
1. Hockey—Social aspects—Canada. 2. Hockey—Canada. I. Title.
GV848.4.C3P644 2006   796.9620971   C2006-903495-8

Editing by Derek Fairbridge
Cover design by Naomi MacDougall & Peter Cocking
Front cover images: © Andy Clark/Reuters/CORBIS (top);
© Reuters/CORBIS (bottom second); © Reuters (bottom fourth)
Interior design by Naomi MacDougall
Printed and bound in Canada by Friesens
Printed on acid-free paper
Distributed in the U.S. by Publishers Group West

We gratefully acknowledge the financial support of the Canada Council for the Arts, the British Columbia Arts Council, and the Government of Canada through the Book Publishing Industry Development Program (BPIDP) for our publishing activities.

IT IS A SIMPLE fact of life in Canada that hockey, directly or indirectly, touches virtually everyone. Whether we're playing or watching the game, reading about it in the newspaper, listening to sports talk radio, seeing a stack of hockey cards at a garage sale, or driving past a road hockey game on a quiet street, the game is every bit as much of our cultural fabric as the loonie, Parliament Hill, the Laurentians, the toque, poutine, Peggy's Cove, Smarties, or the letter zed.

For those Canadians who do not play the game or who don't watch *Hockey Night in Canada* with fervour and who couldn't care less about who wins the Stanley Cup (Lord help us, do such folk exist?!), everyone knows someone—a neighbour, a colleague, a friend—whose kids play, who has season's tickets, who lives down the road from a former NHLer, or who has some connection to the sport. When people joke about the smell of hockey equipment, we know what they mean. When we see kids play hockey on a tennis court, we know the extent of their passion. When we see a grown man in the middle of summer walking to a bus stop with his stick slung in the straps of his equipment bag, looking like a kind of Canadian hobo, we know what he's all about.

In big cities, many Canadians enjoy the opera and the symphony, the theatre and the movies, and, in this country, a trip to a hockey game fits in nicely with those cultural interests and intellectual pursuits. In small towns, the Canadian winter impels kids to don the proverbial skates, play shinny on the proverbial frozen lake, run for the proverbial hot chocolate after finding a proverbial warm place to thaw. These are the images and anecdotes of childhood and adulthood that we pass on, generation after generation. They existed yesterday and today and will exist again tomorrow.

Canada's relationship with hockey began with a geographic and meteorological fact—we have a white and snowy winter, and when it gets cold, we get ice. That's how the very game of hockey began, and we took to it with pre-lapsarian pleasure. As the game grew and developed, every aspect of it became a part of our lives. The mounds of Zambonied snow that sit behind arenas in the middle of the summer speak to this. The Eaton's catalogue with table lamps, bed sheets, and bath towels adorned with the logos of NHL teams are likewise manifestations of how hockey is represented in even our most non-hockey of daily accoutrements. Ads in the paper that mention a "hat trick" of sales at the local furniture emporium also speak to this. Popular players promote cars and clothes and beer and every other kind of merchandise from milk (Doug Gilmour) to Viagra (Guy Lafleur). And then, of course, there is Tim Hortons®. The Hall of Fame Maple Leafs defenceman, now long dead, lives on in the taste buds of millions of Canadians every day who gulp his coffee and savour his doughnuts.

Hockey is not just a sport and it's more than a passion; it is an ingrained part of who we are, how we live our lives and go about our business. Grown men play the game until they are too old and their bones too brittle to endure the rigours of skating. More girls and women play in Canada than anywhere else in the world. Hockey books, hockey cards, hockey videos, hockey posters, and hockey pucks are part of kids' bedrooms from coast to coast and are stashed away in nearly every family basement or garage. "Hockey helmet" is a way to describe a particular coiffed look. No one would know what vulcanized rubber is were it not for the puck. Indeed, the game has a language all its own, from "slot" to "cherry-picker," and "lid" to "hat trick," words that have become part of our everyday vocabulary in and out of the arena. According to a recent poll conducted by CBC, Don Cherry, Wayne Gretzky, and Paul Henderson are among the greatest Canadians in the country's history, every bit as famous as great prime ministers, scientists, artists, and activists.

There is an artistry to the game, both a ferocity and a beauty that make hockey appealing. It's creative but played at breakneck speed. It's played before an enthusiastic crowd, but it's improvised, not scripted, and the outcome is never truly known until the final horn. It is very much a thespian game that develops character and plot. To the players, hockey demands qualities that are unique from—but essential to—life off the ice. It is a game that demands teamwork and builds relationships. It requires the tolerance of pain that develops inner strength. It is a fast game that demands mastery of hand-eye coordination. It is a contact game that requires not just strength but body smarts and assiduity on the fly, as it were. It is a game that includes the mentally strong and the emotionally weak, the sportsman and the cheap-shot artist, the hero and the villain, the brave man and the coward.

Hockey players walk among us—they are like us. They are not overly tall like basketball players; they are not beefed up like football players or juiced up like baseball players. They are essentially average size and weight. What separates them from us is that they are in meticulous physical condition and have incredible speed and strength—and they have an indefatigable will to win that the average person simply does not possess.

Any personal love for hockey begins in childhood and as such it is a family sport first and foremost. Also, it is a sport that demands that parents drive their kids to the arena for early morning practice. It is a sport that is handed down, one elbow pad at a time, one story at a time, one game on *Hockey Night in Canada* at a time, from father to son, from big brother to little brother. It is like church on Sunday morning, a ritual that inhabits our every breath and our children's breath, too.

This book is an attempt to define the collective history of the sport. As such, it is subjective. It is based on experience as much as knowledge, passion as much as encyclopedic thoroughness, daily lives more than hypothesis constructed in a classroom or laboratory. It's about memory and recollection as much as research. It's about people, moments, and objects that together characterize the sport, from its origins to its present-day existence. The culture of hockey is not one-dimensional. It affects music and fashion, science and politics, education and business. Hockey is about camp and kitsch, boys and girls, farms and cities. You cannot live in Canada without being touched somehow by hockey. And, yes, that is a good thing.

ANDREW PODNIEKS, Toronto, August 2006

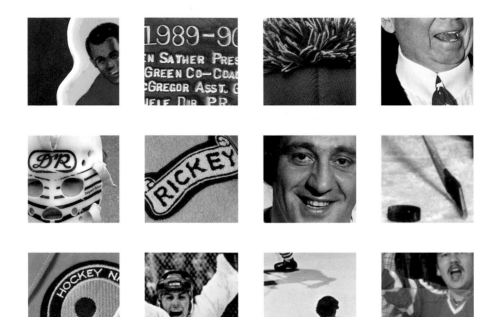

A Canadian
SATURDAY NIGHT

HOCKEY *and the* CULTURE *of a* COUNTRY

ANDREW PODNIEKS

The PUCK

Few objects look as harmless while stationary as they do volatile while hurtling through the air as the plain black puck.

IT LACKS THE technical wizardry of the golf ball, the hand-sewn care of the stitched baseball, the leather crafting of the football and soccer ball, but no other sport's object has been as consistently made for as long as the glorious black puck.

The puck is of a higher aesthetic quality than the lowly ping-pong ball or the inconsequential squash ball, and it is more masculine than the effete tennis ball, which changes shape when hit. The puck is the only black object in the major sports (because it is played on a white surface), and the only thing that changes shape after contact with it is the goalie's glove, the defenceman's shin, or the forward's dental plate. And the puck is just the right weight. It's easy to hold in the hand, flip harmlessly in the air, and stickhandle on ice, but shoot it and it becomes a little black UFO dangerously hurtling this way and that.

Oh sure, American TV tried to change things by introducing pucks that would be illuminated by a digitally generated red-hot streak on screen (the FoxTrax "smart puck") because American viewers (according to TV executives) had difficulty following the basic, black Canadian puck, although they had no trouble with the baseball, the tennis ball, or even the golf ball.

The puck is part of daily life in Canada. You see pucks in stores, in basements, at garage sales. You see them sit lifelessly in buckets or flying right at you on TV. You can give souvenir pucks as presents, or collect them for yourself by the hundreds and thousands, each with a different logo.

Also known colloquially as the "pill," "biscuit," "disc," "boot-heel," and "rubber," the puck is vulcanized simplicity. But then there is the knurl. *Knurl?* Yes—all those little bumpy things along the side of the puck meant to make it easier to handle with a stick. A golf ball may have dimples, a tennis ball, fuzz, and a baseball, its distinctive red stitching, but the puck has its own distinctive marks, the knurl, by definition a series of bumps or knots. Cool.

IT'S THE EARLIEST extant photograph of an indoor hockey game. This image of the Victoria Skating Rink in Montreal, taken by the renowned studio of William Notman & Sons in 1893, is to hockey what hieroglyphs are to ancient Egypt.

This majestic photo is testament to the early game. We see there are no "boards" to contain this game except for a short wooden riser extending just a few inches above the actual playing surface. Fans gather right at the edge of the ice to enjoy the spectacle without fear of injury because there were no slapshots in those days, no bodychecking in the sense that we know today. Notice also the elaborate decoration, the bunting along the balcony, the flags from the ceiling, the banners spanning the interior. The rink was a place for gala balls and pleasure skating much more than it was for hockey games.

We can learn so much about the game itself from this image. There are fourteen players on ice—seven a side. They wear distinct uniforms up top (to denote teams) but similar white bottoms with high socks. There is no noticeable protective equipment being used except for their gloves, which look only slightly sturdier than winter mittens. The goalkeepers stand in front of their respective nets like kids on a pond playing shinny, with no fear of "raisers" coming their way. Everyone uses the same brands of skates and sticks. In the middle of it all stands the referee, dressed in suit and bowler to indicate both his importance and the importance of the event.

The sticks bear more of a resemblance to field hockey sticks than to our longer contemporary sticks, and the goal posts are merely poles stuck into the ice, with no crossbar. Lines for faceoffs and offsides are nowhere to be seen, giving the indoor rink the outdoor feel of a frozen lake or pond. This was a much simpler, gentler game than what evolved in the coming decades, and as such gives us pleasurable insight into hockey's origins and earliest methods of play.

The goalie hardly looks ready to face an Al MacInnis slapshot, but this is how the game began.

RIDEAU HALL

Lord Stanley's love of hockey played at Rideau Hall led to his idea of a trophy for the sport.

Hockey itself owes a debt to government—more specifically, to the governor general's office, which, in 1888, brought Lord Stanley and his family from London, England, to Rideau Hall in Ottawa. His five-year term altered—and defined—the history of the puck-chasing game. In Lord Stanley's day a backyard rink was constructed on the grounds of Rideau Hall (where a rink still exists today), and the governor general fell in love with hockey despite knowing nothing about the sport prior to his arrival in the nation's capital.

At the end of his tenure, in 1893, Lord Stanley donated the Stanley Cup to Canada to be presented annually to the best amateur team in the country. The parameters of the competition have changed, but the introduction of the trophy gave hockey teams a common goal and helped create a structured environment whereby leagues and playoffs determined the best team in the land.

Soon after Lord Stanley's silver donation, amateur leagues sprung up and matured, professional leagues then took over, and teams in the U.S. started playing in Canadian leagues. Out of this expanded interest came the NHL in 1917. From that developed an inextricable relationship between the Stanley Cup and NHL that started in 1927 when the Cup's trustees gave the league full control of the trophy.

The symbolic importance of Rideau Hall—the idealized Canadian residence—setting up a skating rink in its backyard cannot be overstated. If Rideau can have a backyard rink, so can any other Canadian home. If Lord Stanley loves hockey, so should we. If his daughter, Isobel, can play on a women's team, so can any Canadian girl.

By embracing hockey, and by giving the sport a trophy, something to strive for that raised the prestige of the game beyond simple backyard shinny, Lord Stanley helped define our unified identity and spirit. As an outsider, he recognized our love for the game and sought to help us develop and nurture it. We should all play it, celebrate it, and appreciate it. To this day, we continue to follow Lord Stanley's lead.

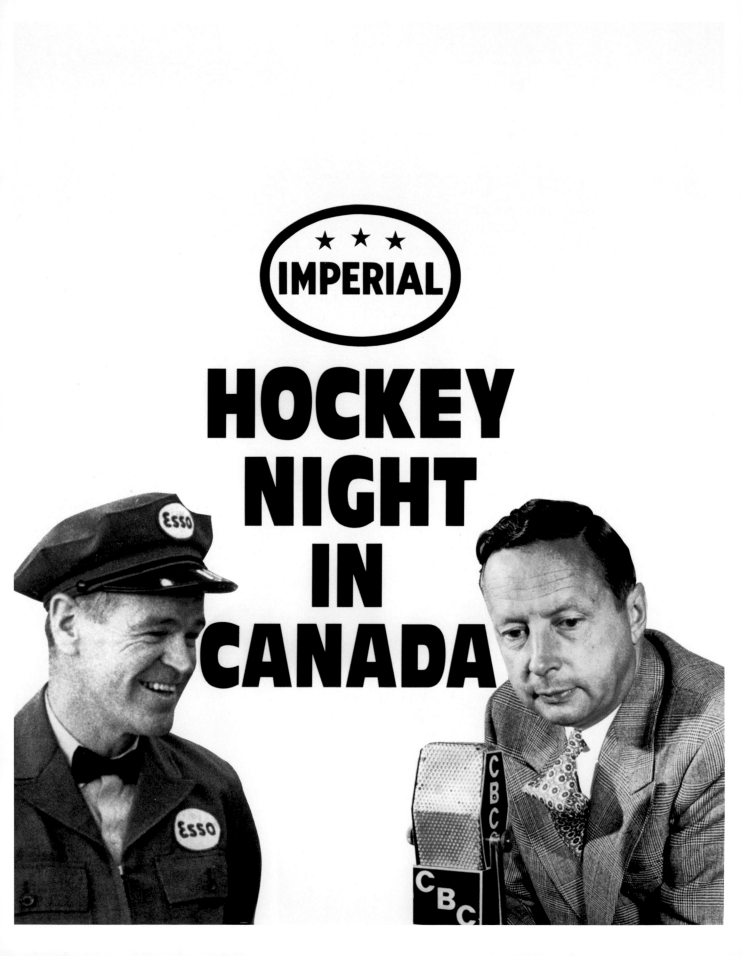

The THREE STARS

THE THREE-STARS selection is a long-standing tradition that grew out of nothing more than a commercial for a gasoline sold by Esso in the 1950s called "Three Stars." The three-stars selection remains an important part of the game-going experience. No matter what the score, you're not supposed to leave a game until you see the three stars take their curtain call, especially when the home side wins and will likely claim at least two of the three selections.

Even in shinny, the three-stars custom remains important. Come off the ice after a game with friends and someone will likely say, "so-and-so got the first star for his play." Kids at the end of a road hockey game will also holler, "and the first star is . . . !" with the fervour of Foster Hewitt.

In the old days, the first star was introduced first, but the current approach is to start with the third star and work upward, to build excitement and drama leading to the naming of the game's best player. Different players, of course, acknowledge the hockey beatification in different ways. No one was more exciting than "The Entertainer," Eddie Shack, who used to skate out to the faceoff circle at centre ice, pirouette with a hockey player's sense of balletic grace (that is, little balletic grace at all!), stop on a dime, then race back whence he came. All the while, the crowd roared mightily.

Other players barely step onto the ice before retreating to the dressing room. Visiting players rarely make an appearance, knowing they are more likely to get booed. There is usually one exception. Players on the visiting team who were once stars on the home team make sure to skate out to acknowledge the applause that is as much in honour of past contributions as that night's particular efforts. Of course, in a tie game, the home side usually gets two of the three stars, but that's to be expected. The three-stars selection gives every game a memorable ending—even if it no longer fills gas tanks.

> Today, we know the naming of the "three stars" as a time-honoured tradition, but originally it was simply a brand of gasoline promoted ingeniously by Esso.

ST. LAWRENCE STARCH COMPANY

Stan Mikita was never Mr. Smiley on the ice, and here his open mouth barely suggests pleasantness, even when posed.

IMAGINE PROFESSIONAL hockey fifty years ago. It was the age of innocence. There was Maple Leaf Gardens in Toronto and the Forum in Montreal. Foster Hewitt was the radio proxy between NHL players and hockey's citizenry. Imagine being a kid back then, following your favourite team and favourite players but having almost no idea what they looked like! You never got to see a game at the Gardens, and Hewitt was too busy with play-by-play to give physical descriptions.

That's where the St. Lawrence Starch Company stepped in. To promote its Bee Hive Corn Syrup, the company produced portraits the size of birthday cards of every NHL player—120 in all!—that it would send free to your door, one at a time, if you mailed in three box tops from St. Lawrence products. Needless to say, every kid wanted every picture.

Each card featured a staged, on-ice portrait of a player, usually with a stick and a puck, skating toward the camera. Some were in colour, many in black-and-white. Most had fake wood frames for borders, and many had a fake wood border of what was clearly a *real* fake wood frame!

The players back then always looked much older than their age. They had stern expressions, even when they were smiling. They seemed suspicious of what they were being asked to do—pose—as if by doing so they revealed something about themselves that they didn't want to, like tribesmen from the Brazilian rain forest who feared their souls would be stolen if they were photographed.

Today, you can go online and download a colour, game-action photo of any player in the world, but back then Bee Hive was your one and only Google for hockey images. Once you had the cards, you could look at them while you listened to Foster call the game, and by so doing you got a fuller sense of what your hero looked like while he played. It allowed one medium—photography—to dovetail with another—radio—to create in the mind's eye a kind of personal television. There was beauty and imagination in that inner collaboration that we no longer have.

STAN MIKITA

M OST NATIONS are defined by their politics and social history, but it's not very often in any country that these characteristics are defined in part by a sporting event. Such was the case, though, on March 16, 1955, when Montreal Canadiens star Maurice Richard was suspended by NHL president Clarence Campbell for the remainder of the 1954–55 season as punishment for hitting linesman Cliff Thompson during a game in Boston three nights earlier.

The day after Campbell invoked the suspension, the Canadiens hosted the Red Wings at the Forum. Campbell attended the game to make clear that he would not be intimidated by Montreal fans. By the end of the first period, however, Detroit had built a 4–1 lead, and at intermission all hell broke loose. Fans showered Campbell with debris and refuse, and a smoke bomb exploded near his seat. Officials suspended the game, but the violence spilled into the streets. Rioters stayed up all night wreaking havoc in downtown Montreal—breaking windows, toppling cars, setting fires, and causing the kind of chaos one would normally associate with civil strife in a war-torn country far away.

For years Richard had complained that the league hated him because he was French Canadian. He believed Campbell was out to get him, and with this incident, Richard claimed, the NHL president finally found his opportunity to strike a death-blow to his competitive heart.

Richard was the people's hero in Quebec, not just because of his ability to score goals but because he came from a poor, French-Canadian family of eight children, and he fought like hell to get to where he got. Throughout life, he never caught any breaks. He saw only discrimination against the underclass, and he saw Campbell and this suspension as another manifestation of this.

The people took to the streets in support of their hero who happened to play hockey, but the political overtones went beyond the rink: it was us (French Montreal) against them (English NHL). It was a political event more than a hockey event.

The Forum in Montreal on the night of March 16, 1955—when politics and sport clashed head on.

The STICK

WHEN FATHER David Bauer, coach of the Canadian National Team throughout the 1960s, gave Pope Paul VI a hockey stick in 1964 during a visit to the Vatican with Team Canada after the Olympics, Il Papa held the blade under his chin while the butt end rested on the floor—such was his lack of rudimentary understanding of our most common of sporting accessories.

Had Father Bauer had a lengthier audience with the Pope, he could have told his holiness that the Canadian hockey stick contained a *Da Vinci Code*'s-worth of information that to the outsider was as mysterious and complex as the Opus Dei.

At the top of the shaft, there is a stencilled name flowing downward, usually of an NHL player. This tells you that the "pattern" of the stick is exactly what that player actually uses in games. There is an "L" or "R" to indicate whether it's a stick for left-handed shooters or righties. There is a number—usually a 5, 6, or 7—that indicates the lie of the stick, that is, the angle created when you put the blade flat on the ground. Also, inscribed on the shaft of the stick is the company name—CCM, Sherwood, Victoriaville. Each company produces many styles, and each style has a name—"Professional," "Hat Trick," "All-Star." There are those mysterious coloured bands of plastic near the blade that indicate what year the stick was made, what kind of wood was used, sometimes even where it was produced.

And then there is the blade. A big hook generates a shot with more speed, but less accuracy. Some blades curve just at the tip, or heel, though most have a gentle curve in the middle somewhere. The flex is also part of the stick's character. Some shafts are heavy and inflexible; some are light and snappy ("good whip" is the way to describe it).

A hockey stick is no different from a violin or a piece of fine furniture—it is the result of craftsmanship. But the best stick is the one that has lots of goals in it, and those are hardest of all to find.

Simple in design, the stick is an object replete with complexity and information that belies its main purpose—to shoot and pass a puck.

O<small>H, SURE</small>, the mother country can claim that "hat trick" is a cricket term that's been in use since 1868 to refer to a bowler's taking three successive wickets. Dear rickety England can go on to claim that "hat trick" was soon enough adopted by association football and used to celebrate the scoring of three straight goals by a player. But everyone in Canada knows that the term gained its widest audience through hockey and, more particularly, through Sammy Taft.

Taft was a haberdasher on Spadina Avenue in Toronto, and it was he who established a literal connection to the term "hat trick" by awarding a new hat to any NHLer, Leafs or visitor, who scored three goals in a game at the Gardens. This was the early 1950s, the very apex of the Original Six era when goals were hard to come by, so it's not as if Sammy were giving out fedoras left, right, and centre.

Over time, the term became fashionable in everyday parlance for any situation in which a three-count was accomplished. An MP went for a hat trick if he won his third term in office; any three great buys at a department store were called a hat trick of sales; a famous person who had a third child scored a hat trick of kids.

When a campaigning politician uses a term like "hat trick," what he's trying to communicate is, "I'm a hockey fan. I'm just like you. Vote for me, and you vote for someone like yourself." When someone uses the term in conversation, he's trying to fit in, talk the talk, establish his own credibility.

There is nothing more awkward than a non-hockey person trying to engage in hockey talk and getting the terminology wrong. So, if you want to talk hockey, don't say, "He scored three goals," or "that goal into the empty net gives him three tonight." No. You're better off to say, "He scored a hat trick," or "that empty netter completes his hat trick." Then you sound like you know your hockey.

> Players who wanted to save a few bucks merely had to score three times at the Gardens to get a free chapeau—easier said than done.

"SOUVENIR PROGRAMS!"

AFTER YOU'VE had your ticket ripped by the usher at the turnstile as you enter an arena, your next step is to find the man hollering, "Souvenir programs!" Once you buy a program, you have authenticated your visit to the game and acquired a piece of your life's history.

The hockey program is no different than the program you keep from the opera, symphony, or theatre. It provides you with information about what you are watching as well as interesting tangential information. It's also something you show your friends as proof that you were there.

There is something magical about that program as time goes by. It marks a place in your life, like a Polaroid, that you can instantly recall through that particular reference. You can look through the program ten years later and see who played in that game, identify players who went on to play bigger or smaller roles with other teams. You recall with a wistful smile with whom you went to the game, a friend who remains close or someone who has since passed out of your life. You recall where you sat—Golds or Greys, great seats or up in the rafters. You recall where you went for dinner beforehand or what you did after the game. You recall where you were working or what you were doing during that time in your life, recall how you came to get those seats.

Chances are, you keep all your programs in one place, and this latest is merely the most recent addition to your life's library of ephemera, along with the ticket stubs, matchbooks, and expired passports that tell you more and more about your life as the years pass. That night that you actually went to the game was merely a moment; with time, it becomes history. And the program is a document of this, a testament to a part of your life that is gone. "Those were the days when..." you tell yourself wistfully as you look at the cover, knowing you can never go back.

The souvenir program not only adds to the pleasure of the game-going experience, it provides enduring proof of the visit itself.

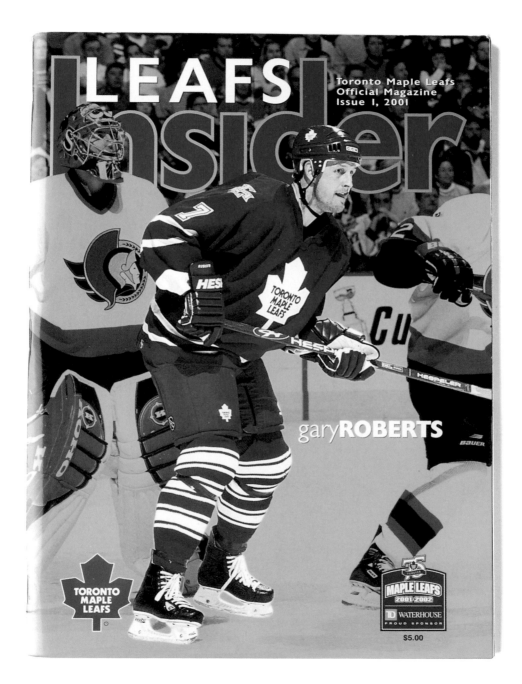

LEAFS
Insider

Toronto Maple Leafs
Official Magazine
Issue 1, 2001

gary**ROBERTS**

TORONTO
MAPLE
LEAFS

75
FOREVER
MAPLE LEAFS
2001-2002

TD WATERHOUSE
PROUD SPONSOR

$5.00

THE IDYLLIC image most of us have of the Foster Hewitt era is of a family huddled near the wireless, listening to the great man's introduction ("Hello hockey fans...") and then his call of the game itself. The picture is indelible in the mind's eye. Dad in his big old armchair. Mom on the couch, knitting, or in the kitchen tending to some dishes; little Billy kneeling on the floor so close to the radio he'd go blind if it were a television; and, his little sister, Sue, drawing on foolscap, or playing with her dolls, somewhat bored. Can you see Dad in this picture with a beer in his hand? Not then.

Now picture various modern permutations of game night in the big city. Dad heads to a bar right after work to watch the game on the big screen with his buddies. His wife is out having sushi with girlfriends; the kids are over at someone else's house playing Xbox. In this picture, you can be sure Dad is having a few cold ones.

Look at any current beer commercial on television during a hockey game or at a print ad in a program. Beer drinkers are you-'n'-me guys who, by virtue of the brew in their hands, attract only the most drop-dead-gorgeous women.

Beer companies use hockey games to purvey their product to a key demographic. The same guys who are in those bars watching the game and watching the beer ads are the same ones who want to meet those women. The beer ads portray a dream night with the boys—watch the game, have a few beers, and look for the ladies at intermission or on the way to the washroom. It's a great way to spend an evening. For the beer makers, it's a great marketing opportunity. Give them beer and a game, and their purchasers will come back for more and more.

And, hey, is it just coincidence, or is a beer bottle shaped just like the Stanley Cup but without the bowl on top? Or is it the Cup that's shaped like a silver beer bottle?

Is there any aspect so tangential to hockey that has become as much a part of the game-watching experience as beer? Eh?

CHICLETS

How can you look at Bobby Hull the same way after seeing this antique plate that fit comfortably into his mouth?

THE ENDURING stereotype of a hockey player is a young man missing his three front teeth. In a way, it's an image both disgusting and appealing. We all watch other sports and say, "I could hit a baseball like that" or "I can make a free throw or put the ball on the green, too." But how many people say, "I can slide in front of that slapshot with my face and lose the front row of my teeth just like he did"? Not that many. Loss of teeth is a real life sacrifice. It's giving up the ability to eat steak or smile in a party photograph at a summer get-together.

Hockey players call lost teeth "Chiclets" to make fun of something that is definitely not fun. Taking a stick in the mouth or getting hit by a puck with such force that teeth fall out is a sacrifice we don't think sports should ask of us, and this commands our respect for hockey. More amazing, players are expected to go to the dressing room after losing teeth, see the team dentist for an examination and clean up—then get back on the ice. Miss a shift or two, perhaps, but that's all the sympathy the sport will allow. In real life, the trauma of a lost Chiclet requires days of emotional suffering and untold anguish in a dentist's chair. In hockey, that time is truncated in the same way a speeding puck moves faster than a bank transaction.

These days, equipment is better and more protective than ever, players are wealthier, and arenas are bigger, but loss of teeth is still a common occurrence in the world of hockey. We recall frightening pictures of a toothless Bobby Clarke skating with the brawling Philadelphia Flyers, but we also know that Dany Heatley, a star of the modern game, skates in the NHL and walks the streets with one tooth missing from an on-ice mishap that cost him a Chiclet. The loss of teeth always has been—and always will be—part of the game. No wonder Bobby Hull's "falsies" sold at an auction for more than $700.

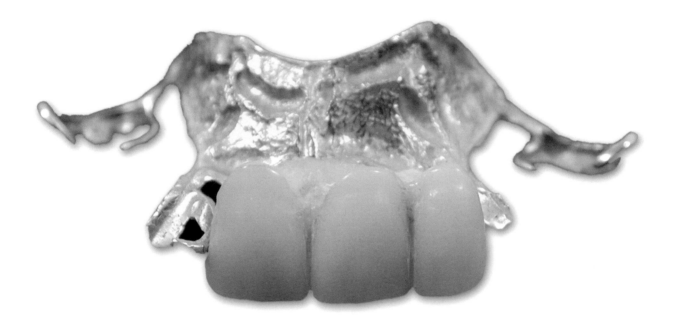

TABLE-TOP HOCKEY provides a number of indispensable benefits to the lives of hockey fans. It's endlessly adaptable. It is a game you can play with one friend, or even two or three. Some hardcore players practise alone, working on sophisticated breakout plays and passing combinations with a mania for strategizing that would be the envy of Gary Kasparov.

Table-top hockey is great for hand-eye coordination, for visualizing, for planning. It's chess played at lightning speed. It's the rec room's Battle of the Bulge. It's part coordination, part strategy. Also, its skill requirements are independent of the real game. That is, just because you are a good hockey player on ice does not mean for a second that you will master the table-top version, and just because you can't skate worth a darn doesn't mean you're a lousy table-top player. Sometimes just the opposite is true.

Its relevance to life also depends on how competitive you want to be and how seriously you take the game. You can piddle around with the sticks without caring, or you can hunch over the bonsai-arena and play with the fire-in-the-eyes intensity of Maurice Richard. Perhaps the former is for a less-skilled friend, someone younger, your disinterested sister who's doing you a favour by playing. The latter you might save for school friends you want to humiliate, who taunt and tease you, who push you to do your best.

The game also teaches you about the fundamentals of hockey. You learn the roles of each position, learn how the players interact when you try to make passes from the corner with your winger to the centreman charging straight ahead to the front of the goal. Some table-top aficionados take their goalie most seriously of all and can have him make great saves by deftly moving that short, small stick from side to side as their opponents try tricky passes and fancy plays. You must learn to counter attack, play good defence, get the puck, and then move quickly to offence before your opponent has time to make the opposite adjustment himself. That's hockey.

> You don't have to be a great skater to play table-top hockey—in some cases, the opposite is true.

BOBBY ORR'S KNEE

This terrifying apparatus kept the greatest player in the world playing as long as he did—which still wasn't very long.

A SIGNIFICANT part of Bobby Orr's mythical stature comes from the fact that his knees were so ravaged by injury that he was forced to retire much earlier than time would normally have allowed. Although Orr quit finally in 1978 after playing a few games with Chicago, his career actually ended in 1975 after just nine full seasons. In retrospect, many say his career ended "tragically."

That word has unique meaning for an athlete because he gets to live two lives. "Tragic," after all, refers to death, and in one sense it is apt because the knee injuries caused the death of his career. In his other life, though, Orr lives on, off ice, working in the game, eating, breathing like the rest of us. Orr sacrificed his post-career health for the game he loved, for the game he played beautifully, poetically, recklessly.

Orr didn't play it safe. He didn't go easy, let up, or skate less than all out. He flowed like Baryshnikov, shuffled like Ali, and continued hell-bent and all-too-briefly like Caravaggio. He left nothing in the dressing room, and when he stopped playing he left nothing in his hockey bag, only this knee brace that is frightening, sickening to look at. The great tragedy is that if he played today, any of his knee injuries could be fixed quickly and relatively painlessly with arthroscopic surgery.

Denis Potvin may have played more games than Orr. Ray Bourque may have amassed more points, and Paul Coffey may have scored more goals, but none lives in our imagination the way Orr does. To this day, a defence-man who takes the puck end-to-end is described as making a "Bobby Orr rush." To put an arrogant defenceman in his place, scouts and general managers continue to say simply, "he's no Bobby Orr." Orr is our hockey myth who played so beautifully you can't believe it unless you saw him live. He was a hero who gave his life to the game. That he lives and breathes today is secondary.

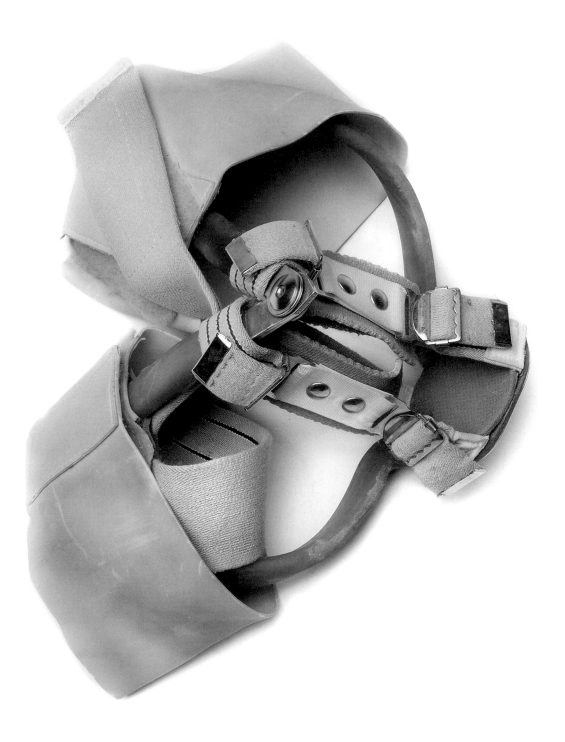

HER FACE IS unknown to almost all Canadians, and her name elicits more grunts of total indifference than drop-jawed admiration. Still, one of her tunes has been dubbed Canada's second national anthem. That, of course, would be the theme music for *Hockey Night in Canada,* the sacred Saturday night ritual that has defined this country for more than half a century.

Dolores Claman is the composer's name, and although the ditty in question is a modest 40 years old or so—pray tell, what did *HNIC* play before she wrote the theme song?—it is as recognizable a piece of music, a piece of Canadiana, as anything that exists in this country. Claman wrote the tune in 1968 for the Mclaren ad agency in Toronto at a time when *HNIC* was trying to brand itself as a more identifiable entity. This effort included, among other things, the announcers' crisp, powder-blue jackets with the *HNIC* logo, of a simple stick and puck, stitched to the breast pocket.

Every episode of *HNIC* begins with the theme song, its horns and drums heralding another exciting evening of hockey for fans from coast to coast. Go into any bar, stand on any street corner, walk into any office in any city in this country and hum those notes—you don't even need the proper recording—and the overwhelming majority of people will be able to identify that tune. Like all things that are popular, its simplicity is what makes it so effective, that and its constant coursing into our brainwaves week after week, year after year—even night after night during the playoffs.

The notes are the musical equivalent to Foster Hewitt's, "He shoots! He scores!" Most every Canadian can say with surety that, "I grew up with that music." It's like a snowy day in January or a frozen lake, or Bobby Orr, Gordie Howe, and Wayne Gretzky rolled into one. And it crosses all boundaries of race and religion, region, and culture. To steal from the beer ad, "It is Canadian."

In the modern spirit of going retro, maybe the CBC will introduce its own "second jacket" and bring back the powder-blue original.

How is it that a doughnut shop has entered the psyche of a nation with such Stanley Cup–like success as Tim Hortons®? The product is now so much bigger than its namesake player that the hockey connection is no longer the lure for customers.

In his pre-cruller life, Tim Horton was one of the best defencemen the NHL had ever seen. By the time he died in a single-car crash the night of February 21, 1974, Horton had played more games on the blueline than anyone in league history. He won four Cups in the 1960s with the Leafs and was inducted into the Hockey Hall of Fame in 1977.

In 1964, the entrepreneur in him decided to open a coffee and doughnut shop in Hamilton. It was a success, and soon one branch after another opened, first in southern Ontario and then across the country. They, too, were successes, so the owners in the post-Horton era of the business expanded the menu to include sandwiches, salads, and novelty soup bowls which you could eat after you had sucked back the contents therein.

Today, at intermission in NHL rinks across the country, Timbits® players (little boys and girls) skate out to play a mini-game on a big sheet of ice. Fans love it, and kids realize a dream by playing on NHL ice. That's branding worthy of Three Stars gasoline.

Cruise down any main street in Canada and you'll see a Tim Hortons®. Walk any distance along a sidewalk and soon enough you'll see a crushed Tim Hortons® coffee cup underfoot. Drive along any stretch of highway strewn with those depressing last-gas exits and you're sure to see the cheery Tim's signage.

In the 21st century, Tim Hortons® is a proudly Canadian success in the battle for caffeine and quickie-food dollars. It may have gone from being owned by a lone, Canadian hockey player to being traded for on the Toronto Stock Exchange and New York Stock Exchange, but the people who buy the doughnuts and coffee and Timbits® have always been Canadian. It only makes sense that someone by the name Tim Horton once played hockey.

The coffee cup is more recognizable today than the player whose name graces it.

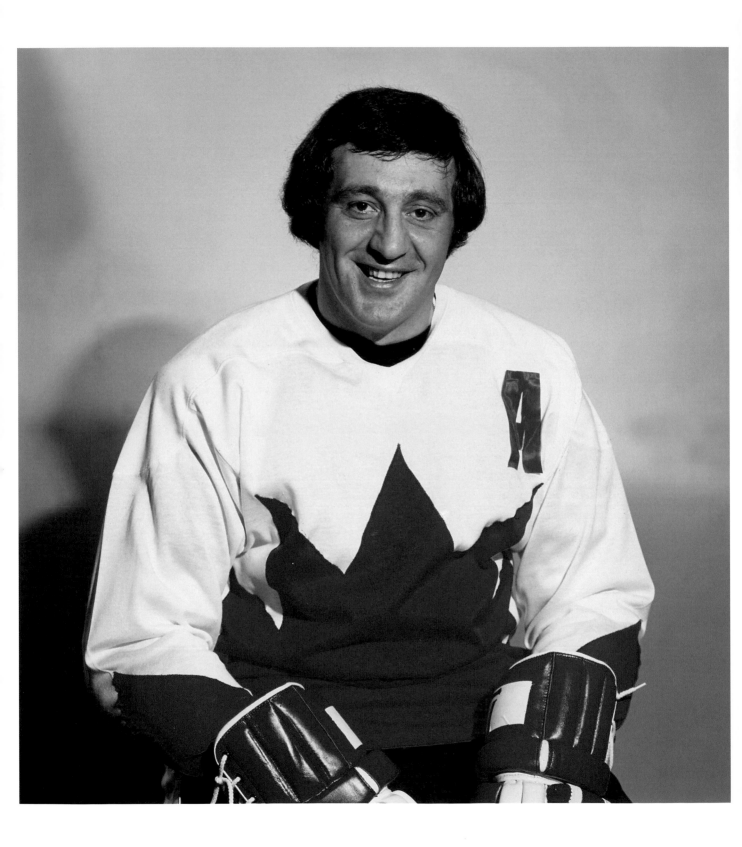

THE BOOING began less than two minutes into the game when Canada's Bill Goldsworthy took a stupid penalty. It got worse when the Soviets scored, got worse again when Goldsworthy took another penalty later in the period. The booing intensified when the Soviets made it 2–0 with another power-play goal.

By the time the Canadian players left the ice 5-3 losers in Vancouver on September 8, 1972, after Game 4 of the Summit Series, they were booed into the dressing room. Coming off the ice, Phil Esposito was interviewed by CTV announcer Johnny Esaw and produced one of the great speeches in Canadian history, a speech that the players wouldn't actually hear for weeks, but one that would inspire the nation's people to take pride in themselves and to support, not deride, their country's team.

"To the people across Canada, we tried. We gave it our best. For the people that boo us, geez... all of us guys are really disheartened and we're disillusioned and we're disappointed in some of the people. We cannot believe the bad press we've got... the booing we've gotten in our own buildings... I cannot believe it. Some of our guys are really, really down in the dumps... Every one of us guys, 35 guys that came out and played for Team Canada, we did it because we love our country and not for any other reason, no other reason... And I don't think it's fair that we should be booed."

Esposito's words struck the very core of the nation's relationship to hockey, our ingrained belief that we were the best, and by much more than just a little bit. Espo's sweat-soaked disappointment and disgust was palpable and forced all Canadians watching to feel shame for their negativity and lack of support.

By the time the series resumed in Moscow on September 22, however, the people had heard the message. Canada's dressing room overflowed with telegrams and letters of support. Luzhniki Arena pulsated to the sound of, "Go, Canada, Go!" and the hero's welcome the team received upon its triumphant return to Canada sealed the greatest moment in our sport's history.

Espo's words— shocked, vituperative, prideful—resonate to this day for their spontaneous sincerity.

"HENDERSON HAS SCORED FOR CANADA!"

WE ALL KNOW the details of "The Goal." Game 8. Luzhniki Arena, Moscow. September 28, 1972. Thirty-four seconds left in the game. This was not only the most important goal in Canada's history, it's the subject of what remains the most important photograph in hockey history as well. How important, after all, could the goal continue to be if we had no visual documentation of it?

There is no doubt that this moment in Game 8 defined hockey for Canada, put the sport in the cultural pantheon beside the paintings of the Group of Seven, the novels of Mordecai Richler and Robertson Davies, the works of creators of every sort. Yet the truth is that without the recorded images of this goal, we would have far less to cling to—our imaginations couldn't do the event justice if we didn't have the game footage or the still photos. Imagine praising a great painting we cannot see or a great novel we cannot read.

Despite the importance of this moment, only two photos of the goal exist—one taken by Denis Brodeur and this shot by Frank Lennon. It is these images, and the TV footage with Foster Hewitt screaming his simple yet immortal words, "Henderson has scored for Canada!," that go so far in making this moment so enduring, so much a part of our heritage and our communal soul.

The image, shot at the precise moment the celebration of the winning goal began, is rich with information. Henderson is facing the camera, arms raised, mouth open wide with joy. Looking at the photo, we put words into his mouth: "I've scored! I've scored!" He's being hugged by Yvan Cournoyer, a smaller man who hugs Henderson as though he were Mary Magdalene hugging the feet of Jesus. In the background, we see the fallen Soviet goalie, the great Tretiak, who has succumbed to the skill of democratic Canada, who has been felled by the resolute fight of the Canadian team, who has been laid low, silenced, vanquished by our ever-so-slightly greater hockey army.

The very essence of Canadian joy is expressed through Henderson's wide-open mouth as he celebrates the greatest goal ever scored.

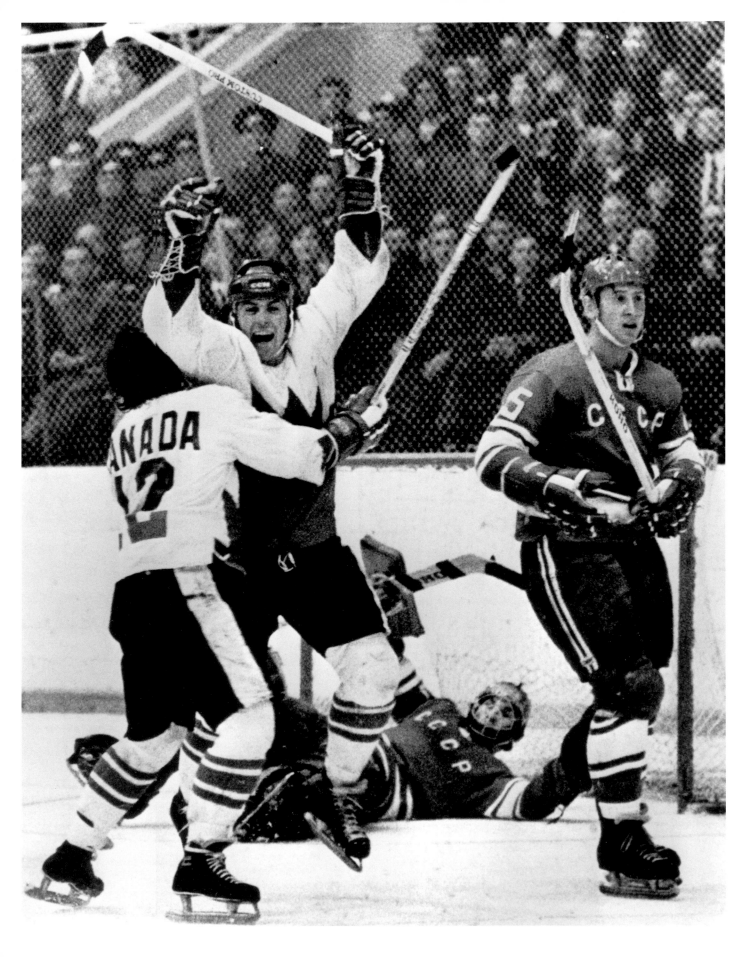

STOMPIN' TOM

AND THE HOCKEY SONG

Also including THE CONSUMER, THE PIGGY-BACK RACE, THE CURSE OF THE MARC GUYLAINE, THE LAST FATAL DUEL, BLUE SPELL, SINGIN' AWAY MY BLUES, THE MARITIME WALTZ, GASPE BELLE FAYE, WHERE WOULD I BE?, TRUE, TRUE LOVE, YOUR LOVING SMILE, MR. ENGINEER

Capitol

To MOST Canadians, Stompin' Tom Connors is famous for one thing.

Hello out there, we're on the air, it's hockey night tonight...

If the *Hockey Night in Canada* theme song is Canada's second national anthem, then "The Hockey Song" comes third (or, perhaps, fourth, after Anne Murray's "Snowbird").

Tension grows and the whistle blows and the puck goes down the ice...

As a small boy, Stompin' Tom was taken from his mother and placed in Children's Aid, then adopted by a New Brunswick family whom he lived with until age 15, when he began hitchhiking his way back and forth across the country, working odd jobs, picking at his guitar at every stop.

The goalie jumps and the players bump, and the fans all go insane...

It wasn't until 1973 that he released the album "Stompin' Tom and the Hockey Song," but the title song immediately captured the imagination of the country on all levels—musical, sporting, cultural.

Someone roars, "Bobby scores!" at the good ole hockey game...

Stompin' Tom was wildly popular and his music sold well all across the country, but in 1979 he returned the six Juno awards he had won to protest what he felt was poor federal support for Canadian musicians. It was a strong symbolic message from one of the nation's leading (singing) voices.

Oh, the good ole hockey game, is the best game you can name...

The original album cover features a then-contemporary photo from a game between Toronto and Montreal (Ken Dryden in net for the Habs) with all the logos removed. The title tune is easy to remember—as are the lyrics—and the twangy, gravelly voice of Stompin' Tom has made this a memorable slice of musical life in Canada, which continues to be played in hockey arenas across the country and, indeed, around the world.

And the best game you can name, is the good ole hockey game.

A Toronto-Montreal game on a Saturday night—does hockey get any better?

The GOALIE MASK

In the 1970s the mask made the man, and Gilles Gratton's mask was manly in a way Jacques Plante could not have envisioned in 1959.

I N CANADA in the 1950s, there were no more barbaric working conditions than in hockey, where goalies were expected to play with no protection for their faces. This went on until 1959 when the Montreal Canadiens' Jacques Plante stood up with the anger of an oppressed labourer and said, "Enough!"

To be sure, in the old days only two or three players on each team were capable of unleashing hard shots, but those goalies still fell to the ice and routinely found their head precariously near skate blades. In truth, pucks weren't as dangerous to goalies' heads as much as stray sticks and wayward skates.

The bravery of hockey goalies in the Original Six era helped create hockey's reputation as a sport for only the toughest of the tough and fiercest of the fierce. Goalies were not just stoppers of pucks; they were heroes, warriors, crazy men who risked life and limb to prevent that little black disc from crossing their goal line.

When we see Johnny Bower today, face long healed from a career's worth of cuts and stitches, we don't think of him as a great goalie or a Cup winner. We first remember him as a goalie who played without a mask. Being a goalie was about bravery first and foremost because if you weren't brave, there was no way you could ever hope to stop the puck.

In Plante's case, his coach, the legendary Toe Blake, loathed the idea of his goaltender wearing a mask in games because it suggested to the other team that his goalie was a coward. If he had been anything less than a future Hall of Fame goalie, Plante would have been demoted to the minors by Blake. Plante knew it. As brave as he was playing without a mask, his most courageous act might have been defying Blake and setting a new path for goalies, who today are still considered brave for their work—just not nuts.

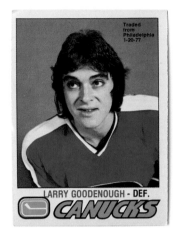

Traded from Philadelphia 1-20-77

LARRY GOODENOUGH - DEF.
CANUCKS

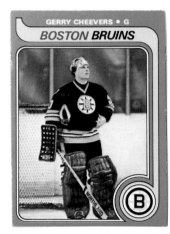

GERRY CHEEVERS • G
BOSTON BRUINS

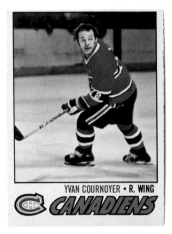

YVAN COURNOYER • R. WING
CANADIENS

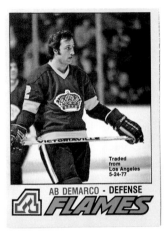

Traded from Los Angeles 5-24-77

AB DEMARCO - DEFENSE
FLAMES

BERNIE FEDERKO • C
ST. LOUIS BLUES

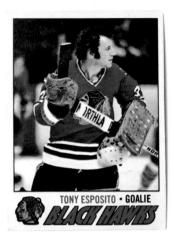

TONY ESPOSITO • GOALIE
BLACK HAWKS

BORJE SALMING • D
TORONTO MAPLE LEAFS
2nd Team ALL★STAR

AL HAMILTON • D
EDMONTON OILERS

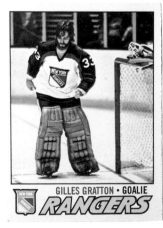

GILLES GRATTON • GOALIE
RANGERS

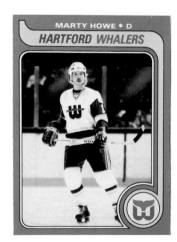

MARTY HOWE • D
HARTFORD WHALERS

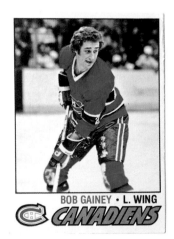

BOB GAINEY • L. WING
CANADIENS

COLLECTING HOCKEY cards was a rite of passage in the pre-Internet days of innocence for any young Canadian boy.

A pack of hockey cards was a magical entity. First, of course, there was the gum. Pink, coated in sugar and about the size of a big Band-Aid, it authenticated your purchase somehow, even though it was extraneous to the real reason you bought the pack. You popped that brittle slice into your mouth, maybe even licked the white, powdery sugar off the top card for good measure. That gum tasted great the first few chews, but within seconds it had lost all flavour.

On the back of each card, you got the player statistics and sometimes a little cartoon with a piece of trivia about the player: "John has a BA in philosophy"; "Paul is a chef from the Bonn'Homme school in his off time"; "Tom once caught a 216 lb. mackerel fishing in Lake Skugog."

Your objective, of course, was to collect all players from all teams, but in order to do this you needed two essential things. First, you needed the checklist card, the most important card of all because it assigned numbers for each card and told you how many cards were in the set. The second thing you needed, of course, were friends who also collected, because without other kids to trade with you couldn't possibly get the whole set. Sometimes you'd trade one for one, easy card for easy card—you know, the ones that seemed to come in almost every pack. Other times, you'd have to give up three or four cards to get a tough one.

In order to assess the worthiness of a friend's collection, you had to go through his stack of cards muttering "got him, got him, got him, need him, got him, need him," flicking the "need him" cards aside for negotiation, passing the "got him" ones into the receiving hand.

It was all plain and simple good, clean fun. Except for the sugary gum.

Even in 1979–80, a Gretzky rookie card was hard to come by. Today? Almost impossible.

SLAPSHOT

Lovers of space adventure have *Star Trek* and *Star Wars*. Goth lovers have the *Rocky Horror Picture Show.* Martial arts fans have Bruce Lee movies, and kids have their repertory of Walt Disney classics. Hockey fans have *Slapshot,* that ridiculous Hollywood movie about a down-and-out, gooning team in the 1970s, the Charlestown Chiefs of the Federal League, modelled after the Johnstown Jets of the East Coast Hockey League. The movie was written by an American (Nancy Dowd), directed by an American (George Roy Hill), and starred an icon of American movies (Paul Newman, as Reggie Dunlop). Geez, even the bespectacled Hanson brothers were American. Nevertheless, the movie is the unofficial *Casablanca,* as it were, for Canadian hockey fans.

The Hanson brothers have become cult figures far beyond *Slapshot*'s fight scenes, as this action-figure set attests.

The lines can be quoted and the characters mimicked by any puck-lover north of the 49th. Who doesn't remember the opening sequence in which goalie Denis Lemieux explains the rules of play in his thick French-Canadian accent to an uninitiated American sports show host? It climaxes with his classic definition of a penalty: "You go to the box, y'know, two minutes by yourself, and you feel shame, y'know. And then you get free."

What about the demented Hanson brothers preparing for their brawling antics by wrapping their hands in tinfoil, and doing so with the same attention to detail as Steve Yzerman taping his stick or Joe Thornton tightening his skate laces? Who can forget the bloodied Hansons lining up for the national anthem after having started a massive, pre-game donnybrook?

Of course, as many people hate the movie as love it because it glorifies violence and parodies the worst aspects of the sport. Purists argue this is why Americans don't like the game, as a nation, and this movie simply represents the game as the average American sees it. Those who love the movie say, loosen up. It's a comedy. Either way, what is most clear is that Canadians don't have a Hollywood-style view of the culture of hockey, or if we do, the perfect hockey movie has yet to be made.

48

PETER PUCK was the anthropomorphic puck creation that explained the game to a generation of hockey fans (albeit for only nine original episodes plus countless re-runs) during intermissions of hockey games. Created by broadcaster Brian McFarlane, Peter Puck had arms and legs that poked out of his round, corpulent form, and he had a squeaky voice that was part Saturday-morning cartoon, part Foster Hewitt. He had a cherubic smile that was the same orange colour as the official NHL shield. He wore skates so that he could slide across your TV screen quickly, and he wore white hockey gloves to keep his hands warm while he lectured.

Peter was innocence dressed in vulcanized rubber. He was kind and smart—boy did he know his hockey inside out! His vocabulary was more limited than Dr. Seuss's, yet he could explain even complicated rules, such as offside, with ease. He never stuttered or stammered, never forgot what to say, never made a mistake.

Peter Puck was Bugs Bunny for hockey fans, an early cartoon version of "Coach's Corner." When intermission rolled around during the weekend matinee game on NBC, you never went away to do something else; you stayed riveted to the TV knowing your rubber action-figure friend was about to make another appearance, give a new lesson, summarize a new chapter in his hockey life.

Peter appeared in real life in mascot form during the taping of "Showdown," another great intermission feature of the 1970s featuring the best NHL players of the day showing off their skills on *Hockey Night in Canada*. He was on lunch boxes, posters, T-shirts, pens, soup bowls, piggy banks, and buttons. If you were only the luckiest kid in the whole wide world your birthday cake featured Peter Puck rendered in icing wishing you a happy birthday. The Peter Puck Fan Club was something to be a part of—if your parents allowed. And there was the Peter Puck stuffed toy that you could talk to and play with or hug in bed as you fell asleep dreaming of winning the Stanley Cup.

The friendly cartoon character takes a big slapper in the rear to explain a point for fans.

OUR NATIONAL ANTHEM

Think about how many times you have heard "O Canada" in the last year and in what contexts. Probably everyone hears the anthem on Canada Day, but the rest of the year?

The anthem surely is most associated with games broadcast on *Hockey Night in Canada*. "Ladies and gentlemen, will you please rise and join [fill in a name] in the singing of our national anthem." The deferential crowd stands and sings, or stares into space while the notes fill the air, and traditionally the last line (the last two or more if it's the playoffs) are drowned out by ever-increasing cheers in anticipation of the opening faceoff.

Today, the distinction of most famous "O Canada" performer must certainly belong to the man who sings before the Ottawa Senators' home games. Lyndon Slewidge, a police constable with a rich baritone voice, sings with operatic grandeur and child-like joy each time out, ending his performance with a nod and a wink and a thumbs-up to the camera.

However, enter the terms *"Hockey Night in Canada"* and "national anthem" into the Google of our collective memory and surely the first entry to appear is the name Roger Doucet. For many years, he took two steps away from the boards onto the red carpet at centre ice of the Montreal Forum and belted the anthem with an enthusiasm that energized the crowd as much as any Lafleur slapper or Robinson hip check. Like a good hockey player, Doucet performed his duties with a brilliance and energy that resonated with the crowd.

The anthem signals the beginning of the evening's drama. It is the turning point from life outside hockey (get some food, go to the bathroom, make a last-minute phone call) to life *as* hockey (follow the puck, speak only at whistles, cheer at appropriate times, appreciate the play as it ebbs and flows). The national anthem on a Saturday night serves to unify the game-going crowd as it does the country every July 1. A hockey game does not begin with the opening faceoff; it begins with "O Canada."

For many Canadians, life fundamentally changes every spring for the eight weeks of the Stanley Cup playoffs. Workmates, schoolmates, friends, Internet correspondents, one and all set up thousands of playoff pools across the country to make the race for the Cup all the more interesting. *Hockey Night in Canada* goes on air every night for nearly a full month, and poor Peter Mansbridge and his CBC national news take a backseat to the fan-driven, income-generating playoffs.

For the 19,000 or so fans lucky enough to have a seat for any given game, many will dress for the night, not in jacket and tie of days long gone, but in a more modern *commedia dell'arte* for the night's puck play: painted faces, team sweaters, funny hats and over-sized hands, flags waving high in the air, horns that produce a cacophony. Of course, a few libations to tickle the tonsils help the game-going maniac cheer on the home side at higher decibels.

The truly creative fans, however, work for hours at home making their own Stanley Cup to bring to the arena in anticipation of victory. These are the fans who go above and beyond the call of duty. Where would these people be without the miracle of tin foil? How many rolls did they use to make their self-minted Cup, forged from the finest foil from the grocery store?

Like their makers, these homemade Cups come in all shapes and sizes. Some Cups are meant to fit snugly on the head, to free up the arms for other cheering purposes. Some are truly life-sized replicas that have to be carried gingerly in both hands, held aloft in part to cheer on the team and in part to let that fan live out his dream of carrying the Cup above his head. This is as close as he will ever get to the real thing. Some Cups are crude creations with only hints of the curvature of the various bands and shoulders of Lord Stanley's original; others are meticulous in their verisimilitude. All, however, are made from the same substance of motivation—passion.

Making this beautiful tin-foil trophy was a way for this fan to share in the celebration with the players who hoist the real trophy on ice.

The HOCKEY SWEATER

Boys in Montreal revered the great Rocket, even if they knew they could never grow up to be like him.

L IKE A POPULAR nursery rhyme or familiar children's song, Roch Carrier's story *The Hockey Sweater* is brilliant in its simplicity. And like any great work, it is as compelling a story today as it was when first published in 1979. Was it written so short a time ago? Yes, but it has become such an important part of our collective spirit that it's as though its essence were written long before the words were set down on paper.

It is the story of a French-Canadian boy (Carrier himself, actually) who longs to receive for Christmas a Montreal Canadiens sweater with Maurice Richard's number 9 on it, but on that special day he instead finds a dreaded Leafs sweater under the tree! The mistake was made by Eaton's, from whose catalogue the boy's mother ordered the cherished garment. As a result of the mix-up, he has no choice but to wear the Leafs jersey when he plays hockey with his friends. He is the lone wearer of Leafs garb while all his Montreal friends, of course, wear the *bleu, blanc, et rouge* of their Canadiens hero, Richard!

On the surface, it's a hockey story based on the game's greatest rivalry, Toronto versus Montreal. It's about the division of language and culture as well, Toronto representing the centre of English Canada, Montreal the heart of Quebec culture. And then there is Carrier's choice of Richard as the hero, a man many consider to be the first truly "Quebecois" hero, a man who spoke about being a proud French Canadian not only in and of itself but also in the context of being *not* English Canadian. Carrier's story never would have worked had the boy wanted to wear Guy Lafleur's number 10, Jean Béliveau's number 4, or "Boom Boom" Geoffrion's number 5. Great players though they were, they were more "anglicized" NHL stars than the Rocket ever was, and they would have been watered-down representations of both the hockey rivalry and the political metaphor.

The Hockey Sweater

Story by
Roch Carrier

Illustrations by
Sheldon Cohen

ASK ANYONE IN any Canadian city what they would prefer, a Santa Claus parade or a Stanley Cup parade, and the overwhelming majority would likely choose the latter. A Cup parade doesn't happen every year, and the Stanley Cup is real!

A march of any sort is a show of unity, an event in which a disparate multitude comes together for a common reason. Sometimes this march occurs as a demonstration in the name of a social or political issue; other times it's to celebrate a cause or a religion, a festival or cultural event. But the Stanley Cup parade is special because it is unexpected, unplanned, and for many cities as rare as a comet.

Cup celebrations in Canada produce parades that even the great Santa Claus can't match.

The guests of honour at a Cup parade are the players themselves, of course. And to see them in this context—out of battle gear—is strange. They now look peculiarly human and vulnerable. A stitched lip on the ice looks heroic and admirable on a player's sweaty face during Game 7. A stitched lip on a man in jeans looks like little more than the result of a barroom brawl. We see hockey players in sunglasses instead of helmets, T-shirts instead of team sweaters, comparatively naked instead of fully equipped.

When a city wins the Stanley Cup it's like the entire community shares in a lottery win. People come out onto the streets and hug each other, just like the players on ice. Fans rejoice for their years of devotion to the team, a devotion that almost always has been longer and more difficult than what any player has given to a team. The parade is that party which rewards loyalty, a reward for loving not just the game but this particular team. In the end, a Cup parade is like the Olympics: you may host only one in your lifetime, but it's in your heart every minute for the rest of your days.

HOUSE-LEAGUE JACKET

IT'S A STATUS symbol, an identifier, like a pair of designer jeans, a personalized licence plate, or a coffee mug with your name on it. The hockey jacket is every player's dream. It has his name on it, his team or league name, sometimes his number and position, all set in crests made of thick wool—substantial, tactile, professional. A young player cherishes it like it's his birth certificate, and with it he is accepted into the country called Hockey. He is a *hockey player*. See? It's right here.

The jacket authenticates a child's on-ice endeavours. No matter how well or badly he plays in a game, the jacket is there on the hook in the dressing room for him to put on afterward. It always feels snug and warm, and because it has his name on it he takes special care not to get it dirty. You go to the arena and back in it. You go out with family in it. You wear it to tournaments, to special occasions. You never wear your hockey jacket while playing road hockey or doing yardwork. You don't wear it in the rain or at any time you might damage it. It's essentially a boy's tuxedo, not a casual piece of clothing to keep you warm. You wear it to school to identify yourself as a hockey player, and in Canada that identity gives you instant credibility and respect. Hockey players, after all, are quick and fast and strong, part of a select group.

Unlike a tuxedo, however, your hockey jacket is worn when you're at the dinner table, when you're watching television, when you go to bed, when you want to impress a girl. You wear it in the summer and when you go to a friend's house for dinner. It's part of the ritual of growing up as you value things that, come adulthood, are not very important, but at the time are critical to your very existence.

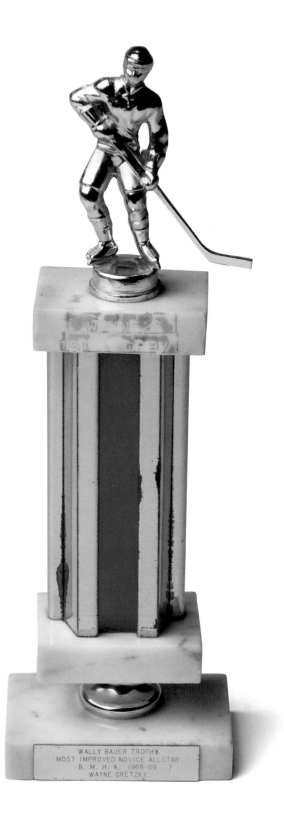

WALLY BAUER TROPHY
MOST IMPROVED NOVICE ALLSTAR
B. M. H. A. 1968-69
WAYNE GRETZKY

From an historical perspective, the Wally Bauer Trophy for most improved novice all-star player during Brantford Minor Hockey Association's 1968–69 season is noteworthy because this was the first of about a zillion trophies Wayne Gretzky won during his illustrious career. From the more general perspective of a child receiving a trophy, it represents a more common celebration.

A trophy is something sacred for a child, a sporting Buddha statue or crucifix—something to be venerated, and never played with or tossed around. It is, perhaps, the only thing a young boy won't throw around until broken! A trophy is to be respected and revered by the receiver because it symbolizes his own personal achievement. It represents reaching an objective. It is a form of congratulation that, not coming from Mom or Dad, is especially important and gratifying for a child. Behold the praise embodied in that golden athlete on his little faux-marble pedestal! You won that of your own merit!

The truth is that almost every child receives a trophy at some point, if not for victory then merely for participation. These common kiddie trophies all look the same: the little plaque displaying the league and, more importantly, the child's name. Later, in adulthood, you might marvel at how something so little made you feel like so much. It's like when you play hockey in a cold, old arena where there is a PA announcer who calls out goal-scorers by name over the loudspeaker. That is something you remember forever.

When you receive a trophy, you put it on the corner of your desk or dresser, or in a window, in the same spot where, thirty years later, in another phase of life, you'll have a picture of your family or objects d'art collected from trips to Nepal or Ecuador.

You grow up and get a job, get married and have children, but one day when you clean out your attic and rediscover your old trophies, you find that you are still proud of them, even though you know they are cheap and their original value has long expired. Like players say after winning the Stanley Cup—*they can't ever take that from me.*

Most Canadian kids have a trophy similar to this first one of Wayne Gretzky's, but none have carried on in the sport with the Great One's success.

The DRESSING ROOM

THERE IS A special bond that grows out of the dressing-room ritual of a father helping his young son get ready for a game. In that dressing room, the child understands the necessity of the equipment, but the logic of putting it on in a certain order is beyond him at his early age. So, the boy sits there, body relaxed, to receive whatever equipment Dad chooses to apply in whatever order the old man deems logical. It's all about trust. The kid knows this equipment is necessary in order to avoid injury, and he trusts that his dad will put it all on properly so that the boy will not get hurt but he will still be able to skate and play without hindrance.

Getting dressed for hockey is exciting. These few minutes of preparation build the drama of leaving the dressing room, walking along the black-rubber mat, the cold, smelly air wafting through the corridor like a gentle breeze, and heading to the clean sheet of still-wet ice. The father is also excited. He looks forward to sitting in the cold stands—hot chocolate always close to his lips, other fathers to his side—and watching his son play, seeing how much he's improved over the last few weeks, seeing how much smarter he is as a player and, by extension, as a young person.

The dressing-room ritual is often silent except for the occasional word from Dad—"push your foot into the skate," "lift your arm," to allow the sweater to come down over his son's head. In that silence is an understanding and a love, because without that help, the boy couldn't play the game.

Once the child is dressed, the boy leaves the room to play and the father is alone, as alone as he'll be the day his son leaves home for the first time. But his heart swells with pride as he heads to the stands to watch the game.

Without Dad to assist, any boy would put his equipment on with scattered logic, creating mayhem underneath the sweater.

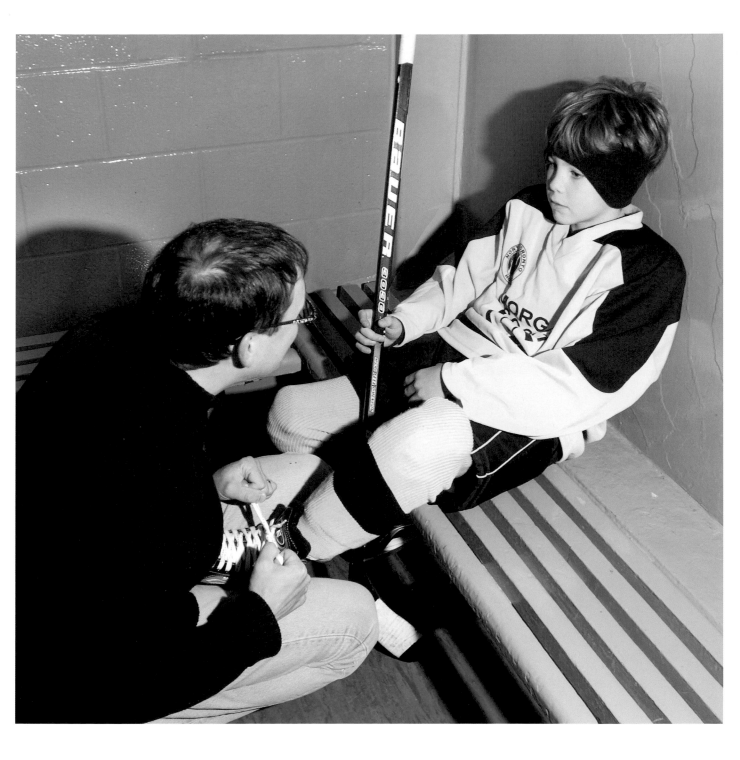

THE GOALIE goes by a number of names—goaler, keeper, puckstopper, target, 'tender. In game-action terms, he's the last line of defence, the best player on your penalty kill, the third defenceman, the man who'll take you to the championship. He is the difference between winning and losing, the difference between a good team and a bad team.

The goalie is usually the most idiosyncratic player on a team. He's often the one who talks to himself or sharpens his own skates or wears the same underwear year after year. He's the one who rooms on his own on the road (or with the other goalie), the one you leave alone before or during a game for fear of upsetting his preparations, the one who is quietest (or noisiest) in the dressing room. He's often just plain weird.

Clever Canadian entrepreneurs have established goalie rental services so that when your shinny team is without one or two goalies (can't find one, a late cancellation, whatever), one will be provided for you, for a fee. A strange guy with pads walks into your dressing room and declares simply, "I'm the rental." Someone pays him, he gets dressed, and the game is great. Paying for a goalie is preferable to shooting at a post or an overturned net or an empty sweater propped up like a lifeless 'tender. In fact, the practice is so common, popular, and essential that there is a television series called *Rent-A-Goalie*. How Canadian is that?

The goalie faces his own private hell every time an opponent skates in over the blueline. A wave of five players comes at him with only one intention—to put the puck in the net. And he's the only one whose sole job is to prevent that from happening. When a teammate is tired from battle and wants a change, he simply skates to the bench. A goalie is in the cage for the duration. No rest, no place to hide, no excuses, no support. As Glenn Hall once said, "How would you like it if 17,000 fans booed you every time you made a mistake?"

Philip Riccio stars as the character "Puker" from the Showcase Original series *Rent-a-Goalie*.

X's *and* O's

I T'S IN EVERY dressing room in every arena, in every town big or small. The chalkboard. It's the ballast, the focal point, the centre of the room. Coaches use it before a practice or sometimes between periods of a game if you're lucky enough to have intermissions. It's where the game is distilled to the symbols of X's and O's. The coach draws set plays in the hopes they work as well on ice under spontaneous situations as they do on the board under controlled circumstances. But by the time he's finished his explanations and drawings, the X's and O's can take on the look of an Einstein equation.

In purely hockey terms, the purpose of the chalkboard is to help each player, and the team as a whole, play better, but in life terms it teaches us how important it is to plan. This might make more sense to us later in life when we're trying to save money for a trip or build a retirement fund. For kids, it's a simple way to take direction and understand that a simple blackboard can be an educational tool. The last stage of understanding how the board works is to go out and try to play according to the coach's plans. After planning comes execution, the final test.

As the coach stands by the chalkboard trying to explain what he wants done, he becomes the conductor of a symphony. What's amazing is that even at the pro level, the chalkboard is still an important tool in coaching, and the players—now 20, 30, 40 years old—are still very much the students, the children being given direction. The arena may change, the league may become more sophisticated, and the stakes of a game higher, but the chalkboard remains the same, five X's and five O's duking it out in two dimensions at the coach's behest in the hopes that when the game is transferred to three, speedy dimensions the outcome will be the same as what has been drawn up in the dressing room.

The chalkboard is usually associated with the classroom, but in the world of hockey the board becomes an educational tool to demonstrate breakout plays, puck strategy, and the like.

O NE OF DON CHERRY's first great ignominious moments came early in the history of "Coach's Corner" when he mocked the Winnipeg Jets' assistant coach Alpo Suhonen. "Alpo?" Cherry sneered. "Inn't that a dog food or somethink?"

In his own inarticulate way, Cherry was making a point. Why, he went on, does the greatest hockey nation in the world need a non-Canadian coach? Nevertheless, the CBC phones rang off the hook. Howls of indignation and protest filled the air as citizens across the country screamed for his head after these derisive comments. Others merely laughed at his humour.

Cherry used another installment of "Coach's Corner" to criticize the size and strength of equipment being worn by the modern player, equipment that has changed from being worn to prevent injury to being worn to inflict injury. Grapes emphasized his point by konking Ron McLean on the head with a current elbow pad and almost concussing his fraternal sidekick in the process.

Cherry got in his hottest water yet when he said the majority of visor-wearing players in the league were French Canadian, a comment that upset many. No one mentioned that, statistically, he was absolutely correct. Instead, his remark was viewed as racist, and the CBC slapped a time delay on his appearance for the next year.

Regardless of controversy, Cherry understands the hockey code, the game played underneath or outside of the rulebook, even if he can't exactly articulate that code. He wants to eliminate the instigator rule, which would increase fighting but provide greater opportunity for star players to shine. Paradoxically, he wants to do away with touch icing because of the risk of injury. He was also the first big name hockey man to endorse the women's game whole-heartedly.

Cherry is something most Canadians are not. He is in your face, unafraid to speak his mind, and seeks the approval of no one. Part hockey philosopher, part Charlie Farquharson, he is beloved by the workingman. And he loves the game as he loves life. That he doesn't quite have the language to explain himself is his greatest foible.

A proud Canadian, a loud commentator, a hockey genius, and a social buffoon, Don Cherry is a bit of everything.

71

BASEMENT HOCKEY

As soon as your parents buy you a mini stick, you start whipping it in the air as if you're taking a slapshot or brandishing a sword. Within seconds, Mom or Dad is saying, "Don't do that!" You hold it by the top of the shaft slapping your thigh with it, running your fingers up and down the blade to test its strength, to see what you can do with it without breaking it.

You get a piece of paper, crumple it into a ball, and start slapping it around. You try a real puck, but realize this will probably break your precious mini stick and abandon the big puck right away. You go back to the paper, add a second sheet to give it extra size and weight. Now, of course, you decide where the goal is going to be. You have to shoot between the legs of a dining room chair or the width of a door jamb. Finally, you smack something with the stick on the wind up or follow through—the wall, your mother's shin, a table leg—and immediately you are told to take your game downstairs.

Of course, you want to play a game and keep score, so you invite a friend over, and, of course, he brings his mini stick. You make two goals and play on your knees to keep the size of the stick in proportion to the player's body. You make mini-hockey rules accordingly: you can't rush the puck past a certain point; only shots are allowed; you can get the rebound only if the ball comes back to your half of the mini-arena. You stickhandle this way and that—quick, quick, quick—and then, *zing!*, rifle a shot on goal. Play to ten and then change ends. At intermission, you go to the kitchen for a drink and talk about the great plays you've just made against each other.

Your knees are red, your fingers blistered, your shirt wet from kid-sweat. You've never been happier in your life. It's almost better than going to a game.

On *The Tonight Show,* Sidney Crosby demonstrates to Jay Leno how he played hockey in his family's basement as a kid.

72

WHEN EDMONTON Oilers captain Wayne Gretzky married Janet Jones in Edmonton on August 8, 1988, it was an event full of celebration. The marriage was dubbed "Canada's Royal Wedding" because he was the nearest thing the country had to a king, this gifted hockey player from Brantford, Ontario, who was shattering records in every season he played. Paparazzi were out in full force, as were gossip columnists and fashion critics to discuss the guest list, Janet's dress, and the banquet at the reception.

Gretzky knew this was not a marriage that could end in divorce a few years later. He knew that he and his wife had to represent the perfect couple, the epitome of happiness and stability, the very definition of wedded bliss. He knew they had to have children, and over time it would be his duty either to raise the next hockey-playing sensation or, like Bobby Orr, protect his kids and keep them well away from any hockey expectations.

The great anxiety surrounding this wedding, though, came from the fact that Jones was an American, born in St. Louis and working as an actress in Los Angeles. Would this marriage turn into another instance of culture drain from Canada to the U.S.? Would Gretzky move to LA, become an American citizen, and raise baseball- or football-playing tykes named Jed or Kalen? That the wedding was held in Edmonton suggested Jones's desire to alleviate these fears, but Gretzky's historic trade to the LA Kings, just twenty-four hours after the kiss at the altar, shattered Canada's false sense of security.

Ever the Canadian ambassador, though, Gretzky became the model spokesman for hockey. Instead of renouncing his roots, he put them on full display. This is who I am, this is where I come from, he seemed to be saying. He continued to set records, the Kings became a Cup contender, and Gretzky made hockey the star sport in a city of stars. In short, he remained Canadian in every way possible.

Like Charles and Diana, Wayne and Janet captivated a nation with their nuptials.

HOCKEY SMARTS

IN THE EAST there was Father David Bauer in Toronto, a man of great spirit, a priest, a hockey coach, a headmaster of St. Michael's College School in Toronto. In the west, there was the pioneer Monsignor Pere Athol Murray in Saskatchewan, who built a school, Notre Dame, during the height of the Depression, that taught academics and hockey with equal enthusiasm.

Both Murray and Bauer felt that the combination of a formal education with a hockey education would create a more complete man because the two disciplines complement each other. The educated hockey player improves his play because he is smarter, thinks more clearly, learns more about discipline, and is better prepared for life after hockey. The student who plays hockey becomes more successful because he learns how to be a team player, learns the vital importance of a healthy physical body to a healthy mind, learns how to take a win with a grain of salt and a loss with pride.

Pere Murray knew that school kids who could play hockey were more likely to become self-motivated. He also knew that hockey was a distraction, a healthy way to take time off from studies. For some kids who didn't like school, hockey was the only reason they went to class.

A young man's mind is as malleable as warm clay. He can be moulded this way or that. The truth is that trying to put a little black puck into a net is therapeutic to the millions of non-NHL-calibre people who have walked our land. It requires desire and determination, planning and teamwork, a need to overcome fear and the development of confidence and self esteem. You must trust others and trust yourself. You must not criticize or judge or feel superior. If you develop these qualities and never play a second of professional hockey, you are still a good hockey player and an accomplished citizen. That's what Pere Murray and Father Bauer both knew when they put hockey and high school together.

Pere Murray was a generous man who knew the value of hockey to education and vice versa.

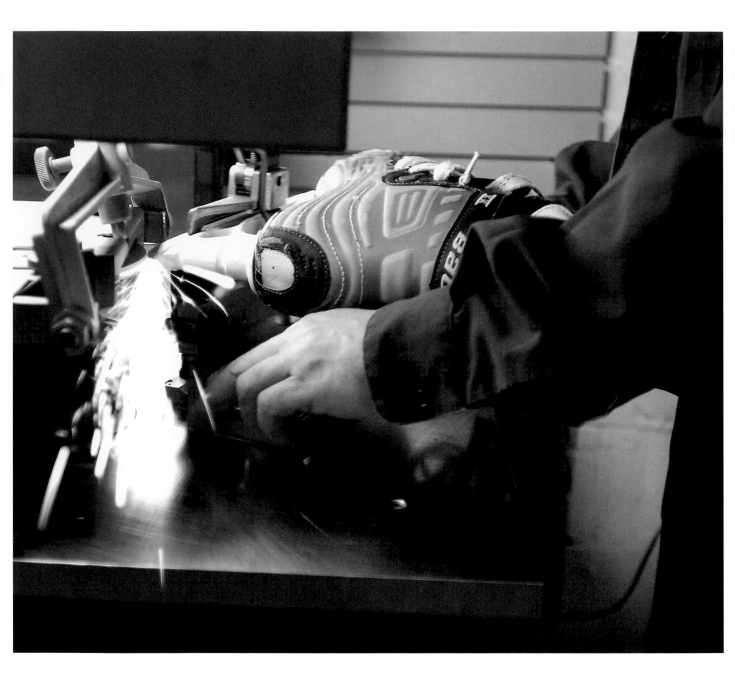

WHETHER IT'S summer or winter outside, it's always only one season inside the arena—the season of hockey. And regardless of what arena you're in, from coast to coast, each consists of the same elements: gumball and candy machines; snack bar and pro shop; water fountain; Zamboni area.

The snack bar sells those rubbery hot dogs with plastic-looking mustard on top, the too-hot chocolate, and the stale popcorn. The pro shop is like a store you'd find in an airport—a smaller, over-priced version of what you get in the middle of the city.

The quality of the arena, though, is defined by the skills of the skate sharpener. If he is worth his salt, you never have to worry about sharp blades. If he's not so good, you have to make a special trip somewhere else to get your skates sharpened before playing. The right sharpener will have a nice, even flow with his hands as he slides the skate blades back and forth along the front of the stone. He'll make the same number of cuts to both blades, and he'll check the evenness of the blade once he has finished. He'll then use a small stone to give the blade that final edge, sliding it in one direction only, not back and forth. A quality skate sharpener is like a barber, tailor, or mechanic—find a good one and you keep him for life.

Wherever you walk in the arena and you see black rubber matting, you know you are near the ice because that's where the players go from dressing room to playing surface in their skates. The black rubber is the Hollywood red carpet of hockey. It gives players a feeling of importance. On a more practical level, of course, it prevents skates from dulling. Walk on wood once in your blades and you'll remember the difference for all time as you are left with dull blades, powerless to turn on ice—except to the exit, where you search out the skate sharpener, who shakes his head in dismay as he takes your skates back to the shop.

A steady hand and keen eye are the skate sharpener's most important attributes—that and a sharp stone.

USED ICE

In summer, it looks refreshing. In winter, it blends well with the real stuff that falls from the sky.

IT'S A STRANGE sight, to be sure, yet a sight so common to Canadians that we don't give it a second thought. It's the middle of summer, heat and humidity making every step heavy and unpleasant. But there, behind the hockey arena, near the doors for the Zamboni, is a mound of snow. It's a sight that is both puzzling and pleasing, the former because we ask how the snow has not melted, the latter because we see this mound and imagine how cool it must be inside.

No, the snow doesn't melt because, in truth, it isn't snow. It's a mixture of various chemicals with some water thrown in for good measure. It is, evidently, impervious to heat in ways in which we are not! It is the only detritus an arena produces (apart from garbage bags full of used tape, broken sticks, discarded towels, empty pop cans).

Hockey is the only sport that produces this sort of sport-garbage from the very material that physically allows the game to be played. After a basketball game, you may have a few wet towels from mopping the floor, but you certainly don't have a mound of wood chippings to get rid off. After football? A bag of grass clippings? Baseball? A disgusting dugout's worth of sunflower seeds, spat tobacco, tossed Gatorade cups?

Hockey's ice surface produces this amazing stuff: used ice. What we see behind the arena is snow culled from the ice surface that is no longer of use. It's essentially garbage, but you can't really throw it out. It's what you skated on perhaps just an hour ago, but now it's just an impermanent sculpture. Lovely to look at, but practically useless. Ultimately, that is its greatest characteristic. We go by the arena in the summer and look at that mound with fondness, with the hint of a smile, with a sense of pleasure. Once the used ice is dumped outside, you can no longer skate on it, but it still serves a purpose in our psyches. We know there is ice nearby, and we are happy.

IT IS QUINTESSENTIALLY Canadian that the more successful our hockey players are, the more humble they are about their accomplishments. Take, for instance, the creation of a museum in the family basement. Players go to tournaments and win trophies and medals. The most successful make their way to championship games, to higher levels of competition, national and international levels of play. Yet for all the prizes they cart home, they take them downstairs and stick them on the basement wall or cheap metal shelving, far out of sight. That wall or shelf, however, is testament to a player's early history, his portrait of the player as a young man. It's a little archive rich in minor hockey history and personal lore, but wonderful as it is, it is not the be-all and end-all of his life.

By putting our early treasures downstairs we say something fundamental about who we are. We are proud of our accomplishments to the point of wanting to "exhibit" the awards, but not so vain as to put them in the family living room for every guest to see. That would be too gauche. We know that while these trophies are important, they are not the Stanley Cup or an Olympic gold medal (which might rightly claim a spot in the aforementioned living room). The basement is the right place for the lesser awards. Trophies and medals give us a sense of accomplishment, of having finished something and done something well, even, simply, of having been someplace at a particular time. Thus, it is right to feel good about receiving an award. Equally, though, it is also right not to feel *too good* because life has a way of taking you down a peg when you feel great. As any coach will say, don't let the highs get too high or the lows too low—solid advice in life as well as hockey.

The humble, not to mention superstitious, hockey player is only too aware of this. Take pride, but don't show off.

Sidney Crosby relaxes in his basement in 2005, surrounded by his trophies and memorabilia.

BROTHERS *and* FATHERS

WHEN LOUIS SUTTER died in the early spring of 2005, the hockey world mourned the loss of the country's greatest puck patriarch. Louis and his wife, Grace, brought seven sons into this world in Viking, Alberta, six of whom went on to play in the NHL at the same time. It was an extraordinary achievement that will surely never happen again, but that it happened in hockey isn't surprising so much as it is revealing. Hockey is the most family-oriented sport in the world, and the Sutters are the Dionne quintuplets of the hockey world.

You need the financial support of your parents to buy the equipment. You need your parents to drive you to your games and practices that, whether in a city, town, or rural area, are rarely within walking distance. You need coaches to teach you and teammates to play with, but more than anything, you have your brothers and father.

Hockey has dozens and dozens of brothers and father-son combinations. Mario Lemieux and Larry Robinson, Denis Potvin, Patrick Roy, and Wayne Gretzky all had brothers play in the NHL. The Patrick family goes back to pre-NHL days in hockey. Ted Lindsay was the son of an NHLer and today there is a whole new generation of up-and-coming NHLers whose fathers played pro: Yan Stastny is the son of Peter; Brian Ihnacak is the son of Peter; Zack Parise's father is J.P. and Brady Murray is the son of Andy. Year after year new brother combinations play in the NHL, everyone from well-known names like Paul and Steve Kariya to lesser known players such as Steve and Dominic Moore.

As for the Sutters, the fact that one family had seven children is special. That they were all boys is remarkable as well. That these farm boys all went on to play serious hockey, six in the NHL, well, that isn't so special as it is, simply, the Canadian way.

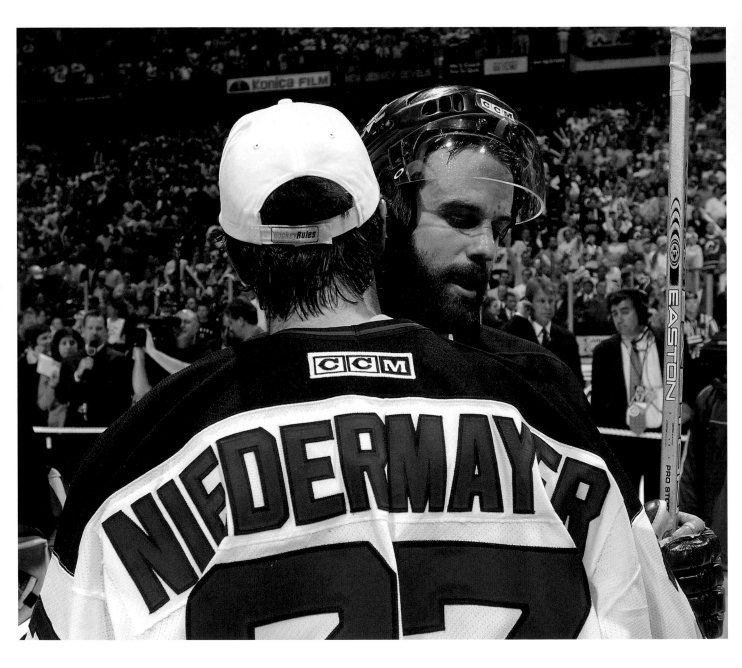

THERE IS NO gesture in sports equal to the end-of-series handshake that hockey players participate in during the playoffs. For four games or more they hit each other as hard as they can. They try to intimidate, overwhelm, defeat. When it's all over, they congratulate each other. They don't always want to, and some boors occasionally skate off the ice before the handshakes, but by and large all players participate. It's a tradition as old as the game itself.

The handshake is part of a life lesson. It takes a big man in defeat to offer words of praise to his victors, and it takes an equally big man to accept those thanks with gentlemanly humility. Part of being a great winner is not just posting the bigger number on the scoreboard—it's the acknowledgement to your opponents that on another day they could have just as easily won.

What occurs during the game is one thing; what happens after is another. Once you've tried your best, in victory or defeat, you must congratulate your opponent. This is a time for disarmament, a time when brothers playing on opposing teams embrace, enemies acknowledge a newfound admiration for each other, stars share a warm respect for other stars.

Most players simply shake each hand firmly and quietly, but you know the goalies say something special to each other about the luck of the game, a great save, or a mutual respect. Likewise, opponents who have once played together as teammates say something that has greater meaning than "good game." The best players, the ones who determine the outcome, and the lesser lights who rise to the occasion, also get fond words from admiring opponents. In the end, once the scoreclock has served its purpose, the players return to the real world where having tried their best is the proudest a player can feel, win or lose.

Rob Niedermayer (facing) hugs his brother Scott, after Scott's New Jersey Devils defeated Rob's Mighty Ducks of Anaheim in the 2003 Cup finals.

Ah, the simple
life through a
Canadian lens. Any
patch of road will
do, so long as you
have a net, a ball,
some sticks, and
a few friends.

Road hockey is a malleable game. It can be played alone or with a dozen people. If you want to play by yourself, all you need is a net or target, a stick, and a ball or puck. The solo version is best played in the driveway where you can place the net in front of the garage door. That way, shots that go wide come back to you quickly. When you're alone, you practise your stickhandling, rocking that orange ball back and forth, twisting, turning, feinting with your shoulders before letting go a shot. You fish the puck out of the net, go to the end of the driveway (i.e., centre ice), and move in on goal again.

If a friend comes over, you can play two-on-the-empty-net, or one person can go in goal. If you play out together, then you move in on goal as linemates, passing back and forth quickly until someone finally whacks home the ball with a quick shot. You go back to the end of the driveway and repeat.

The best game, of course, is out on the road with a group of friends. You only need one goal to play, but two is better. The curbs are your boards, and who in this country has not heard the peal of kids' voices screaming, "Car!" as a car approaches and slows? The ball carrier puts his foot on the ball to stop play officially and maintain possession. The goalies pick up the nets like they're gates at a border crossing and move to the side of the road to let the car pass. They then move their nets back to the middle of the road, and the game continues. You do this until it gets dark, or until the guy whose ball it is says he has to go for home for dinner, or until you're simply too tired. The next day, you play some more.

ONE OF THE joys of hockey is that it's like a great jazz song: it can be interpreted and celebrated in many different forms while remaining faithful to the original. There is no such thing as table-top basketball or three-on-three baseball or road football. Non-ice hockey is celebrated most faithfully on side streets and backroads and laneways. Different equipment is required, for instance, and there is no more famous an accoutrement than the orange, road hockey ball.

Pick it up. It's light as a feather. It feels good in the hand. Now, stickhandle with it. It rolls easily back and forth from the front of the blade to the back. It has a nice smacking sound when you shoot it, and it has enough weight that you can really let fly when you get a chance.

Its most distinctive characteristic, however, is how it feels on the receiving end of a shot. The inventor of this ball must surely have smiled with sinister glee at his choice of material, this durable yet pliable plastic, because you only have to take one shot in the flesh of the thigh to feel its incredible shock of stinging pain.

That damn orange ball sometimes hurts more than a puck, and the next morning when you get into the shower you'll scream when the water touches that red circle of road-hockey pain. That lunar mark on your thigh will stay with you for days, and it will hurt like hell every minute. It's really quite unlike any other kind of pain.

Of course, when you go out to play the next night with those same friends, you play gingerly, afraid of getting hit in the same spot. And, of course, guess what? You invariably *do* get hit in the same spot, and the pain is redoubled and the bright mark on your body is made all the more indelible for the foreseeable future.

Floats like a butterfly, stings like a bee—that's why this ball is great for road hockey.

ROAD-HOCKEY GOALIE

THE ROAD-HOCKEY goalie often puts his pads on at home and slowly walks to his friend's place, waddle waddle. The pads make walking awkward but the goalie feels special because of the way he looks and the noise he makes. No point in telling him it's faster to carry the pads and put them on at his friend's place. He hopes people are checking him out from behind their living room curtains to see him with his mask on the top of his head, his stick held awkwardly in his blocker hand, his glove hand moving back and forth with exaggeration, and his jacket bulky like a chest protector. All in all, a knight in not-quite-shining armour.

When he arrives at his friend's, he puts the mask on next. Light but designed to the latest NHL standards for looks and design, it gives the goalie a sense of imperviousness from serious road-hockey injury. It makes him look like a pro even if he can't stop a beach ball.

Mr. Road-Hockey Goalie adjusts his blocker, usually torn and taped, wiggling his fingers into a comfortable position, shaking it from side to side to cozy it into place. The battered glove is next—more wiggles and a few punches from the blocker into the mitt to ensure it's on properly—and then the goalie picks up his stick and is ready to play.

As he slides from post to post on the snowy road or makes a great glove grab, he'll eventually twist an ankle or scrape a knee. Cries of, "Hang on!" fill the air as everyone comes over and makes sure he's okay.

When it's time for him to go home, the road-hockey goalie takes his mask off, and his blocker and trapper, picks it all up and waddles back home in his pads. He has made the game amazing merely by his presence, his equipment, and his efforts. In that order.

> Any kid who goes to the trouble of dressing like a pro deserves respect, regardless of his puck-stopping abilities.

THE BACKYARD rink can be as primitive or elaborate as you want. Essentially, all you need is a reasonably sized flat yard, water and a hose, and some cold weather, all of which are in plentiful supply in almost every Canadian region. You can simply clear an area, water it, and wait for it to freeze overnight to build a layer of ice. You can professionalize that frozen area by setting up boards, installing nets, hanging floodlights even.

The backyard rink is, first and foremost, a play area. It's a place where friends can get together and enjoy a game of hockey in the comfort of your own home, so to speak. It's hockey room service. Whether you have full-sized goal nets or two boots for a goal is beside the point. You don't need equipment, just a puck. If you don't have boards, you'll improve your eyesight because you will forever be watching the puck disappear into snowbanks and forced to try to find it.

The backyard rink is a great place to perfect the fundamentals of hockey—turning, stopping, accelerating, passing, shooting. There are no bench-clearing brawls in the backyard game, no slashing and hooking, no crackdown on obstruction or trapping defences. The humanity is ever-present because you are aware that it is a game, that your kitchen is right there, that your family is inside, that you are merely goofing around with your friends.

The backyard rink distills the game to its purest essence, its 19th century form of rickets on the ice. It is the Pioneer Village you can create by yourself for your own pleasure, a place you make that takes you back to the game's humble origins when the Stanley Cup was competed for out of doors. Backyard hockey explains the game and provides a near-Biblical context to the game's origins and its importance to the people of the country who are blessed with an imagination to build these magical mini-ponds.

There are no tag-up offsides or touch icings in backyard hockey, but kids still manage to have all the fun in the world.

95

STAMPING *the* CUP

THE TRADITION of stamping players' names onto the Stanley Cup did not begin in 1893 with the introduction of hockey's greatest trophy, but it began not long after and has become a central part of the trophy's prestige ever since. To have your name on the Cup means you are officially part of the game's elite history, one of a small number in hockey's most exclusive club.

The trophy represents so much more than just the NHL. It is a part of Canada every bit as much as Parliament Hill, the maple leaf flag, the Thousand Islands, maple syrup, the inukshuk. It is one of the most recognizable symbols of Canada, one of our most cherished exports, and one of our proudest possessions. It is the epitome of "trophy," the best example of a sports award in the world. When people admire it, they admire it like they would a painting or sculpture, a work of art. The Stanley Cup is our *Thinker* or Eiffel Tower or *Mona Lisa*. It is an object—beautiful, simple, sublime.

We see the bowl at the top, the original gift from Lord Stanley, and admire its craftsmanship. We imagine drinking champagne out if it. We see the body, the heft of it. We realize that you have to be strong and courageous to capture it. We see the names stamped (not engraved) on the barrel, and only then do we really consider it in its hockey context. We look for a name or a team to connect to. We stop randomly and reminisce. There's Gordie Howe. Never saw him play live, but he played for more years than anyone else. Bobby Orr. That was the year he went flying through the air when he scored the winning goal. Pete Kelly. Who was he? Jacques Plante. Look how badly they spelled his name! Where are the '67 Leafs? Where's last year's winner? Where are the five in a row by Montreal? Look at how many names are on it! Every letter is magical, every year a concise summary of hockey history.

The names on the Cup represent a year-by-year directory of greatness. Only the most determined players, however, are given a place in the trophy's history.

EDMONTON OILERS 1989-90

PETER POCKLINGTON OWNER GLEN SATHER PRES. & G.M.
JOHN MUCKLER HEAD COACH TED GREEN CO-COACH
RON LOW ASST. COACH BRUCE MacGREGOR ASST. G.M.
BARRY FRASER DIR. P.P. BILL TUELE DIR. P.R.
WERNER BAUM DR. GORDON CAMERON DR. DAVID REID
KEN LOWE BARRIE STAFFORD TR. STUART POIRIER
LYLE KULCHISKY ASST. TR. JOHN BLACKWELL DIR. O. AHL
ACE BAILEY ED CHADWICK LORNE DAVIS SCOUTS
HARRY HOWELL ALBERT REEVES MATTI VAISANEN SCOUTS

M. MESSIER CAPT. J. KURRI ASST. CAPT. K. LOWE A. CAPT.
S. SMITH J. BEUKEBOOM M. LAMB J. MURPHY
G. ANDERSON A. GRAVES C. MacTAVISH K. BUCHBERGER
C. SIMPSON M. GELINAS R. GREGG C. HUDDY G. SMITH
R. RUOTSALAINEN C. MUNI B. RANFORD D. BROWN
E. REDDICK P. KLIMA E. TIKKANEN G. FUHR

THE MYTHOLOGY of NHL players taking possession of the Stanley Cup for a summer's day has become so compelling that you'd think the tradition was as old as the mug itself. Not so. In fact, this ritual of a private victory celebration is scarcely a decade old.

When individual players have their day with the Cup, though, it has more significance than victors just having a party. Symbolically, it is another NHL fact that drives a wedge between the players of yesteryear, with their miniscule pensions, who made the league what it is today, and the millionaires currently playing who have reaped the tremendous benefits. In the old days, you had the Cup on the ice after the final game and in the dressing room for a few minutes to hold briefly and admire. Then, league officials hustled it back in its case and took it to Montreal where it sat untouched in a vault until the next year's champion was determined.

Since 1994, players have been able to share the trophy leisurely with friends and family, and most choose to do good as well, hiring a photographer to take pictures of fans with the Cup, at a cost, for charity. But as the Cup's worldwide celebrity has grown, the uniqueness of its availability has been cheapened.

The modern player who earns many more millions that his childhood hero holds the ideal of the trophy with the same worth as any player from a bygone era, but he holds the trophy itself with sometimes little more than casual interest. In the early 20th century the mug was left curbside by members of the Ottawa Senators after they changed a flat tire, and it was kicked into the Rideau Canal on another occasion in 1905. But in the last decade it has ended up at the bottom of Mario Lemieux's swimming pool, been dismantled and tossed around by less respectful players, and had all sorts of food—from popcorn to lobster to Jell-O—dumped into its topmost bowl by their friends and relatives where once only champagne resided. All in good fun, but perhaps not quite what Lord Stanley had in mind.

In the last decade, the Cup has traveled to Red Square in Moscow, Wenceslas Square in Prague (pictured here), and virtually every other European capital.

GRETZKY'S RESTAURANT

To get into Gretzky's Restaurant you have to do what Dad said never to do—grab the skates with your hand.

YOU WON'T FIND a Tim Hortons® coffee shop in the chic part of your town. Tim's coffee is the workingman's beverage. Tim's is the local hangout where you pay with the change in your pocket while you hug that folded tabloid under your arm as you add sugar and cream at the little side table with a hole in the middle for garbage. Gretzky's Restaurant in downtown Toronto is the polar opposite. The Great One keeps the possessive apostrophe in his name, and the change in your pocket won't even cover the tip so don't bother counting it out.

Gretzky's is all glam. It represents the modern superstar. In fact, the presence of Gretzky's on Peter Street was so important, and the superstar's influence so powerful, that Gretzky himself managed to get the street name changed from Peter Street to Blue Jays Way to better align it with the strip of road that leads south to the Skydome, where the baseball club plays.

Gretzky's is swishy and upscale. The restaurant up front is where you can drink and dine and watch the game on giant high-definition flat-screen TVs. All around are glass cases full of number 99's sticks and gloves, pucks and trophies, and other artifacts from his one-of-a-kind career. In back is a large open space that has been used for everything from filming TV shows to hosting news conferences and corporate parties. The Wayner goes there all the time when he's in town, usually staying until every kid has an autograph, every granddad a photo.

Over the years many a star or plumber of the NHL has opened an eatery of some sort, from Ian Turnbull's Grapes to Don Cherry's Grapevine, Toe Blake's Tavern and Maurice Richard's Number 9. None, however, has had the drawing power, or staying power, of Gretzky's. That restaurant has found its niche in the party-consciousness of the city, and the name is as popular as ever in the minds and hearts of hockey fans and big-city dwellers. As Timbits® are to Tim's, so martinis are to Gretzky's.

Ask for a hockey story, and everybody in Canada can tell of some connection to the game. You can't help it. You walk into a bar in the country called McKech's Place and find that it belongs to ex-NHLer Walt McKechnie. You buy a new shirt and see Mark Messier's name on the label. You push your shopping cart up to the cash register at the grocery store and see Steve Shutt in front of you. You can never sleep in on the weekend because you have to take your kids to a practice. You learn that another kid can't come to the birthday party because he's in a hockey tournament that weekend. You go to a garage sale and see a road hockey net for two bucks—good condition, too. Your kids keep bugging you to take them back to the Golden Arches, not because of the food but because of the promotional hockey cards. You watch the national news at six and see a big game profiled, an act of on-ice violence reported, a retirement announced. A man arrested for a crime is wearing an All-Star Game sweater or an Oilers ball cap. You pick your mom up at the airport and the entire Leafs team is on the same flight. You drive to a friend's place and en route see a man carrying his equipment to the closest bus stop. To get to a meeting you drive by Bobby Orr Public School, then on your way back to work you take Gordie Howe Boulevard. You turn on the radio and even if you try to avoid it you still hear a snippet of hockey talk on all-talk, all-sports radio. A neighbour makes a snowman on his front lawn and uses a carrot for a nose, puts a toque on his head, and a hockey stick in his snow-arms. You get caught in traffic as fans file into a game from a nearby arena. You go to a sports-themed restaurant and order the Hat Trick Burger and the Power Play Fries. You drive up north and see the sign reading "Welcome to Timmins, Home of Bill Barilko." You're in a corner store with a friend and see an old man who looks somewhat familiar, and your friend tells you that it's Red Kelly. He lives just down the road.

Bob Davidson lived in this anonymous Leaside house for many of the forty-five years he was with the Leafs as a player and scout.

GIVE BLOOD—PLAY HOCKEY

THE CRITICAL distinction between success and failure in hockey is your ability to "do what it takes" to win. This involves not just skill but mental toughness, determination, and a willingness to go through that proverbial wall to succeed. The expression "cuts heal," for instance, is simple, if not a bit oblique, to non-hockeyites, but the message is clear. Don't whine. Don't complain and say you're hurt. Play with pride, with honour, with a ferocity that defines your relationship with your teammates and with the game. Be certain that the pain of defeat, the psychological pain of letting your teammates and yourself down will be far more enduring than a bump or a bruise, a cut or a break.

A team cannot win the Stanley Cup unless (until) it plays *as* a team. No passengers. If you are willing and capable of enduring what is needed to win, you will succeed in a way few people can. This is why great players have such difficulty adjusting to the real world after retiring—they can find no pursuit that pushes them as much (both physically and mentally), and they can find no reward worth pursuing to that nth degree as much as the Stanley Cup.

The brutal truth is that a broken bone can be repaired later. A cut can be stitched—on the players' bench during a game, if need be. A puck is just a piece of rubber no matter how hard it hits you. A bruise is simply a patch of purple skin. A tooth comes out easily and can be replaced just as easily. A pulled muscle recovers of its own accord. These minor injuries should not get in the way of the ultimate dream, the Stanley Cup.

Hockey can prepare you for life. It is a microcosm of life. If you can't play hurt in hockey, chances are in the working world you'll show up late, do your job lazily, phone in sick when you're tired, and never succeed to your full potential. There are inner pains far worse than a few stitches on your forehead.

Cuts heal.

EVERYTHING ABOUT the Zamboni is special. Look at the doors of any hockey rink. There are the two doors for each team's bench, doors for each team at the penalty box, and at one end or in one corner are the doors for the Zamboni. The door-message is clear: the Zamboni is as important as Gretzky or Orr or Howe for making a game great.

As the Zamboni goes around and around, scraping the old snow off, then splashing new water on in one motion, fans watch attentively to make sure the driver doesn't miss a spot. To turn a corner too quickly and leave a crescent moon of snow is simply bush league, unacceptable, the sign of a lousy driver. To finish the flooding with just a thin strip of snow left in the middle of the rink is also intolerable. The driver must finish by flooding a strip just a few inches narrower than the width of the Zamboni's back end, and if he does so, and doesn't miss any spots, he is deemed by the crowd to be a first-rate Zamboni man, a real pro. If he finishes at the far end from the doors, he's also given a failing grade, for he must finish his last lap as he drives off the ice. Everything about the Zamboni's manoeuvres are a representation of ice maintenance and arena operations. These alone distinguish pro from amateur, superstar from minor leaguer, at the Zamboni level of life.

The Zamboni man is also the unofficial mayor of the arena. He oversees everything that goes on in the building. He has the dressing room keys. He can sell you a stick, loan you a puck, or hang on to any equipment left behind in the dressing room. The Zamboni man is the custodian of all things hockey at the arena. When he goes home, the arena is locked and the game is over until the next morning when he returns to flood the green ice. That's Zamboni-speak for the first flood of the morning.

Prior to the 2002 Olympics in Salt Lake City, Utah, Jimmy MacNeil drove his Zamboni across Canada for charity.

LUCKY LOONIE

THE STORY OF the Lucky Loonie from the 2002 Olympics in Salt Lake City, Utah, started with Trent Evans, the head of the ice crew for hockey at that city's E-Center who usually worked the Northlands Coliseum in Edmonton.

Evans placed a Canadian dollar coin underneath the ice at centre ice as a good luck token for Team Canada. Once the players found out—the men's team and women's team—they felt additional inspiration, perhaps even a sense of obligation, and went on to win a double gold for Canada. The loonie was then retrieved by the general manager of the men's team, Wayne Gretzky, and sent to the Hockey Hall of Fame, where the legend of the loonie is preserved for all eternity.

The lore behind a lucky loonie goes far deeper than the Salt Lake games, though. Hockey players are certainly a superstitious lot, a fact attributable not to any loonie-ness in their heads but to a desire for consistency and reliability in a sport that is anything but.

Almost every hockey player dresses the same way before every game. Perhaps it's left shin pad, then right, left skate, then right, perhaps the other way around. Gretzky himself always made sure that when he stepped on the ice for warm-up, his first shot always went wide right. Superstitions are a way to calm yourself before a game, give in to a routine before the ensuing mayhem, do something with a near-religious sense of ritual that always gives you comfort. It's something you can control, something you can do for sure, something you can always rely on.

The loonie at centre ice gave the players in Salt Lake a point of focus, gave them something Canadian in an arena that had few tangible objects to remind them of home. It gave them a goal, forced them to remember who they were playing for, reminded them that everyone back home was counting on gold. That the loonie was there meant little on its own; that the players *knew* it was there meant everything.

This unassuming loonie became a symbol of success in 2002 when its presence underneath centre ice helped Canada win double gold.

JOHN BOWER
18

THANK YOU

WASHROOMS

AP

18TH HOLE RULES

The 18th hole is designed to
resemble an ice hockey rink.
DO NOT, however...
· treat the green as a rink surface
· use slap shots on the surface
· throw dirt on the green

IN THE OLD DAYS, pro hockey players finished the season at the end of one week and started their summer jobs the following Monday. There were virtually no exceptions. Players from rural areas went back to the farm to bring home the crop while big-city heroes went to work for their NHL team owners or small businesses in their hometown.

Players today, of course, are millionaires and don't have to find summer jobs. They don't need the money and they don't have time. They must stay in shape year round and show up for training camp in September in mid-season form. Players of days gone by, by contrast, didn't have the chance to do this. Training camp was when they started to get into shape, and many of the best players were not in peak condition until Christmas. Times have changed.

Retired players find their way into occupations as varied as any section of society. Ken Baumgartner, a fighter on ice for years, moved to California and worked for Goldman Sachs. Derek Sanderson, who squandered his millions on drugs and alcohol, became, ironically, a financial advisor in Boston. Randy Gregg became a doctor, and the Barrett brothers became firemen. Tom Fergus, who had his best years with the Leafs, returned to Toronto after he retired and started a business that makes personalized sweaters, T-shirts, hats, pucks, you name it. Literally.

After years of watching games from the crease, many goalies become television analysts. Other players sell hockey equipment or cars or real estate, just like ordinary folk who never played a game of serious hockey.

Most players of days gone by are hard working, industrious, straightforward. They are our heroes, our sporting saviours. Would you rather buy a car from Jiminy Slick with greasy hair and a crooked smile, or Barry Cullen, who played left wing with the Maple Leafs? No contest. Cullen's name would be on the back of your SUV, a Maple Leafs star on your car! It doesn't get much finer than that.

The signature hole at former NHLer Vic Hadfield's Golf and Learning Centre in Oakville, Ontario, is the eighteenth on the mini-putt course—its hockey-rink design is a real stunner.

POLITICS

Who could have guessed that Frank Mahovlich of the 1960s, Cup-winning Leafs would one day end up in the Senate?

RUSSIA HAS ITS writers and France its painters, England the monarchy and America its Hollywood stars, but Canada looks up to and holds highest its hockey players. These are our heroes, the men and women who do our country proud at home and abroad.

As a result, the political arena has occasionally lured players off ice and to your front step to ring doorbells, preach a platform, or represent a political party at some level of government. The esteemed Jean Béliveau was offered the position of governor general in the 1980s and declined for family reasons.

Béliveau was a model player. He won the Stanley Cup ten times, several while team captain. He played the game with grace, great skill, and sportsmanship, yet he was not to be trifled with physically and could and would defend himself if need be. His character and conduct would have made him a great politician. His qualities were such that you'd believe that whatever he wanted to try, he would succeed.

Not too long ago, Frank Mahovlich was offered and accepted a seat in Canada's Senate, and there were few naysayers in the land. He was to the Leafs what Béliveau was to the Habs, and, as with Béliveau, we recognized in him behaviour of the highest standards. Not surprisingly, Mahovlich responded to the job's demands. He became a model Senator in large part because he had no political agenda, no nepotistic motives. He was everything we wanted out of a politician: he worked hard, was honest, didn't ask for the power given him, and was someone we admire and emulate.

Hall of Fame goalie Ken Dryden became the most ambitious hockey-politician yet in April 2006 when he indicated his desire to lead the Liberal Party. By so doing, he declared his intentions to one day become prime minister.

It's not a stretch to say that we need more hockey players in politics, people who approach their duties with integrity, unwavering determination, and a single-minded purpose to success. No, we don't need the Tie Domis and Matthew Barnabys of the game in parliament, but Ottawa would surely be a better place with a few more Sutters, Hawerchuks, and Dionnes.

Fɪʀsᴛ, ᴛʜᴇ pronunciation. Only a foreigner (read American) would say, "toke." It's "two-k." It's "took" with a soft Scottish accent. It's knitted, and you put it on your head when you play hockey outside, in the cold, in an open space where the winds whip around and make your eyes water and your ears go red and your nose all sniffly. It's both aesthetic and practical, a different kind of headwear that keeps the heat in by clinging its wooly self to the pate.

In the 1920s, there was a Montreal Canadiens player, Aurel Joliat, who wore a toque during games (he wasn't the only one, but he was the best player of those who did). He wore it because he was self-conscious about his thinning hair, but opponents knew if they wanted to get him mad they just had to pull the toque off and watch him go berserk.

Another Habs player, goalie José Théodore, made the toque more famous more recently, at the ɴʜʟ's first outdoor game, in Edmonton, on November 22, 2003, when he tended his goal in full equipment, with a toque on over his mask. A photo of him made every major newspaper the next day, in part for its humour, in part because it captured in one image the Canadian-ness of the outdoor game itself.

A toque means the clap of a stick on frozen ice, the sight of your own breath forming clouds. A toque means mittens and long underwear, a second pair of socks and a turtleneck. It's friends and hot chocolate. It's shoveling snow to make a rink. It's boots for goalposts and throwing sticks in the middle to choose teams.

A toque is to Canada what the beret is to France, the sombrero to Mexico, the Stetson to the American West, and the Panama to Ecuador. It's the helmet to soldiers and the bonnet to lassies. It's Canada's contribution to the universal hat museum. And without it, outdoor hockey would be much less enjoyable.

It's the quintessence of Canadian fashion, the country's contribution to world history expressed in headgear. It's the simple, almighty toque.

SHANIA!

How appropriate was it in 2003 when our own delightful Shania Twain hosted the Juno Awards ceremonies in Ottawa that, over the course of the evening, she dressed in the haute-couture sweaters of the six Canadian NHL teams? There is no more effective or surer way to win over a crowd of Canadians than wearing the city's hockey sweaters, but Shania being Shania, she had the logos and team colours designed in a more fetching way than what is available *prêt a porter* at Eaton's or your team's local souvenir store.

The team logos are each city's flag, really, the most identifiable and simplest way of saying, "I belong to this place." When the Rolling Stones play and practice in Toronto, Mick Jagger will at some point wear the Leafs' blue and white. When Bono plays with U2 at the Bell Centre in Montreal, he'll don the *bleu, blanc, et rouge* of the Canadiens.

What else could Shania have worn to represent the principal cities from coast to coast? Dresses made of the ten provincial flags? Not Shania's funky aesthetic at all! Hockey binds the country together, the city to the country, the east to the west. If you are local or foreign, there is no clearer way of saying, "I love Canada" than wearing an NHL sweater.

But our fair Twain of Timmins went one better. A woman of her savvy was hardly going to wear an actual hockey sweater, the sleeves running down past her fingertips and the hem sliding down to her knees. No. Shania took those logos and made them into something worthy of a catwalk in Milan or an Annie Leibovitz magazine shoot. The howls and screams of delight from the crowd when she came out in each outfit were in part for representing a team and in part for doing so with such élan. The boys loved it—and so did the girls.

THE WORLD POND Hockey Championships, held in Plaster Rock, New Brunswick, is an annual tradition that began not long ago, in 2001. Yet it is such a perfect manifestation of our country, our climate, and our love for the game that it feels as though this tournament has existed for the better part of 150 years.

The Plaster Rock tournament is played on a frozen lake divided into 24 separate "rinks." The sight from above is majestic, truly a mosaic, like a rural scene from a painting by David Milne, William Kurelek, or Jean-Paul Lemieux (in Lemieux's case, for instance, see *Patineurs à Montmorency* and appreciate the connection between that image and this).

The Plaster Rock event was born out of the area's desire to build a new indoor arena, and a government promise to match, dollar for dollar, private contributions to help finance the building. The community banded together and organized a tournament, the profits from which would go toward the arena. A local hardware store provided the pucks. Neighbours brought shovels to clear each sheet after games. Everyone pitched in to make the event a success. It went over so well that long after the appropriate money was raised and the arena built, the tournament carried on. In succeeding years, teams from across the world applied to participate, and now there is a years-long waiting list to play.

The Plaster Rock event is as much a testament to working together as it is a hockey game. It's community spirit realized, like some sort of über-bake sale or maple-syrup festival. It proved that what can be accomplished by many is always greater than what can be accomplished by one. And the means to that accomplishment was hockey, a game near and dear to everyone's heart in that community. It's about friends and friendly competition, and it's a winter festival celebrating nature in the most Canadian way imaginable—playing hockey on a frozen lake. How great is that, eh?

A more majestic tapestry of all-natural, outdoor-rink beauty cannot be found than in this aerial photo of Roulston Lake in Plaster Rock, New Brunswick.

CAN YOU SIGN THIS?

Jean Béliveau
should be
commended for his
legible autograph,
which took a couple
of seconds longer to
write than today's
more impatient stars
take and is a greater
treasure as a result.

Autographs are a strange emblem of personal worth for the holder of the sacred scribble. You ask for an autograph because you see a famous player, at the rink or at the mall or on the street. He obliges, and all of a sudden you have a piece of personal history. You were part of a hockey player's life for a few seconds. You can tell your friends you met so-and-so, and if they don't believe you, you pull out that folded receipt, that magazine, that shopping list or whatever piece of paper you had on hand when you met that famous player. Your friends believe you. The older you get, the sillier the habit becomes, yet you still do it.

An autograph is proof that you spoke to the player, if even just the words, "Can you sign this for me, please?" That meeting, that personal time, is an immeasurably valuable part of the autograph experience. Somehow, for whatever reason, you managed to get this famous player to take a few seconds out of his life to acknowledge you and create a memory for you. That is as important as the document you take home with you. It also means that in the few seconds when you meet the player and get his autograph, the two of you are in the same space, in the same world. You are equals for this tiny morsel of time!

An autograph gives you personal insight into the player. You can integrate into your retelling of the story that he was accommodating and kind or just grudging. Did he talk to you? Did he personalize the autograph? Did he live up to your expectations? One thing is certain: after you have personally acquired a player's autograph, you never look at him the same way again, for better or worse.

Jean Béliveau

DU CLUB CANADIEN et DIRECTEUR de la PROMOTION SPORTIVE chez MOLSON'S

F OR ANYONE obsessed with hockey, it is possible to incorporate the sport into virtually every aspect of your life.

You turn off your Maple Leafs alarm clock at 7 AM, roll out of your Senators bed sheets, and put on your Canucks slippers as you head to the washroom. You brush your teeth using that new Oilers toothbrush, dry your face on the Flames home-and-away set of bath towels, and put on your Leafs PJs before heading to the kitchen for breakfast.

The kitchen is a veritable ode to hockey. You turn on the Tiffany-style Flames lamp to face another day of Wheaties—Hayley Wickenheiser limited edition box, no less. You've got your Canadiens coffee mug (which you set down on the matching Canadiens coaster), your Senators dishes, and Canucks serviettes. You sit on the Leafs bar stool and read the sports section, then dry the dishes with your Oilers tea towels, and, noticing by your Oilers wall clock that the tempus is fugiting, go upstairs and get dressed for work.

Your office has to be comfortable and efficient. Your Maple Leafs mouse pad must be positioned just so, and the matching wastebasket must always be to your right. Your Senators notepad and fountain pen are beside your computer and phone for easy note- and message-taking, and your first order of business is always to look at the entries for that day's appointments in your Leafs daytimer to see what meetings you have and with whom. When you decide to cancel a meeting you're not looking forward to, you flick the top of your Joe Sakic bobblehead and he nods back confirming your decision.

Back home at day's end, you have dinner and watch the highlights from last night's games on the sports channel provided by your local cable package. Tired by midnight, you tuck yourself back under those Senators bed sheets, set your Leafs alarm for 7 AM again, and count Zamboni laps as you fall to sleep, another day of hockey life in the record books.

Only a fanatic would see dental reward in buying this Flames toothbrush with a puck attached. Does it reach all the way to the molars?

RITE *of* PASSAGE

Fans form a sea
of red and white as
Canada's juniors play
at home (Halifax
in 2003, to be
precise) in the most
important under-
twenty tournament.

Y<small>OU HAVE</small> not seen hockey until you have seen Canada play at the World Juniors.

Outside of Canada, the World Junior Championship is a small tournament, an annual event that, when hosted by Finland, Sweden, Russia, even the United States, causes barely a ripple of fan roistering. Only one thing saves the WJC from anonymity—Canada. Fans here go crazy for the stars of tomorrow, the finest players under twenty years of age skating with a whirlwind ferocity and national pride that both defines and defies their youth.

The tournament appeals to Canadians on different levels. For one, there is seldom a controversy about who is on the team. Oh, sure, there has been the occasional player to pass through junior who has snubbed Team Canada. But by and large the players are only too happy to play for their country, no questions asked. Canada's superior management and coaching staff pick the best young players in the country, and for a month around Christmas and New Year's, they represent our home and native land to the best of their abilities.

The difference between professional and junior hockey is never more pronounced than at the WJC. There are no player agents involved in the World Juniors. No free agents, no Group 11's or walkouts or contract demands or performance bonuses or trade demands. No idiotic talk about "small market" and "large market." Canadian fans, players, and television make the tournament a rousing success. Why, even when it is hosted by the U.S., the tournament is played in cities near the Canadian border because most of the fan support comes from the north. When the World Juniors comes to Canada, the enthusiasm reaches a fever pitch. Tickets are hard to come by. Players from other countries marvel at the filled arenas. The atmosphere is charged with unmatched fervour. For the players, it is a rite of passage, a celebration of the final level of hockey before amateurs becomes pros and pristine hockey becomes systemized, before boys become men. It's hockey's bar mitzvah.

THE NAME APPS is legendary in hockey. Syl Apps was a paradigm of success as a player with the Leafs in the 1940s. His son went on to play in the NHL, and now *his* daughter—three generations later—is a star on the international stage with Team Canada, gold medalists at the 2006 Olympics in Turin.

Gillian Apps represents both all that is traditional and all that is changing in the game. Only in Canada, where the game has such a rich tradition as well as a forward-looking commitment to development, could a daughter inherit a father's hockey mantle. The women's sport has grown in this country by leaps and bounds, and we now have heroes named Hayley and Cassie who are every bit as popular to women as Bobby, Gordie, and Wayne are to the long-standing fans of the NHL.

The legitimization of the women's game is reminiscent of something akin to emancipation. With official Olympic status, girls could breathe more easily and say, "We want ice time in arenas around the country. We want equal access, and we want manufacturers to make our own equipment: women's sticks and shoulder pads, sweaters and socks in women's sizes." And the jokes about pink tape? Not funny.

Today, girls in Canada who play hockey get a pat on the back, just like the boys. Girls and boys play together up to a certain age, and they all try their best and have fun. To give girls that chance to play hockey is to give them access to an important social stream where they can exercise, learn team play, feel greater self worth, and become healthier members of society, just like the boys.

Today, Gillian Apps and Jennifer Botterill are a Bobby and Gordie in their own right. They are role models for other girls because of what they have accomplished and what they represent. That Canada's women are Olympic champions twice over also means we can admire them in the context of their own sport irrespective of what the men accomplish on the international stage.

Girls who play hockey now have the Olympics to aspire to at the highest level, while they also have kids' teams and rec leagues of their own, irrespective of the boys' game.

MADONNA *of* THE RINK

The deification of
the NHL player
reaches new heights
in Saul Miller's
painting of a hockey-
star Christ-child and
Mary, the ultimate
hockey mom.

ONLY IN CANADA could the concept of sport as religion work as effectively as it does in Saul Miller's paintings. We take our religion seriously enough, of course, but we have an "open" relationship with our various gods such that Miller can make his point, walk safely through the streets, and be praised or criticized as we see fit. For those who might call this work sacrilege, however, an admirer can counter just by saying, loosen up.

There are three main elements in this composition that take the Madonna-and-child theme and make it entirely a hockey image: the baby Vancouver Canucks player, with skates on; the red line of a rink in the background instead of the oblique rocks as in the *Mona Lisa* or the mysterious, beckoning windows of Vermeer; and, the use of gold-painted hockey sticks as a frame (spray paint, not gilt!).

In any painting, the eye is drawn to the foreground, the central figures, the main theme, but the background always adds to that primary visual message. This red line speaks unmistakably to hockey, and combined with the skates on the Canucks baby Jesus, it's clear this little boy is a hockey-playing saviour!

That Miller exchanges the usual simple cloth clothing of Jesus for hockey togs points to the revered status hockey players hold in our society. What Jesus was two thousand years ago, and the Beatles were forty years ago, hockey players are today in Canada to a good many fans and zealots of the puck game. The players have a power over us of which they are aware. They are sometimes humbled by this power, and they sometimes use it to their own end.

In the end, the image can be interpreted either lightly or seriously. Do we hold our hockey players in Christ-like veneration? Does the sport have too great an impact on our collective consciousness? Are we too worshipping? It's just a sport, after all, not a way of life, like Catholicism. Either way, it's a provocative and profoundly Canadian dialectic.

IN THE credit-card-commercial language of today, you could say that the dream is priceless. It's a dream that can't be quantified, but it's what can make any kid's childhood satisfying. It's the dream of meeting your hockey hero, of seeing him up close, of trying to play like him. The dream keeps the kid out of trouble, keeps him focussed, gives him a reason to wake up in the morning happy, allows him to live the game.

Every kid gets his first glimpse of great hockey players on television. It's a long way away from the faces of the players, to see them play in miniature, to see them being interviewed in close-up but far away. You get a little closer when you go to a game, but still you're also farther away because you don't get the TV close-ups of your heroes. You may be only fifty feet from them in your seats, so you *feel* closer and are emotionally closer, but you're really farther away because you can't see their faces as clearly as on television. Still, watching your heroes in person teaches you so much more about the game than what you can learn from your living room.

When you see your heroes up close, you see your dreams come to life. You are inspired and, in their presence for that fleeting moment, you are as important as they are, because they are spending their time with you (and you with them). You are of equal status for that one breath, a breath you hold in your dreams for days and months and years, a breath you take with you wherever you go and whatever you do.

That's why you buy the posters and put them on your bedroom wall. That's why you collect their hockey cards and memorize their statistics and know when their birthdays are. That's why you wear the same sweater number and use the same kind of stick that they do. You dream, perchance to play. And if it doesn't work out, you've grown up with a solid role model and given yourself a chance to succeed. That is what hockey can do for a kid.

> If only every kid could see his hero so close for even a few seconds. If only every hero could make each kid's dreams come true!

The SKATE

THE WORD "hockey" can, of course, refer to the NHL or to Team Canada, but it also refers to house-league hockey, rep hockey, girls' hockey, indoor and outdoor hockey, road hockey, summer hockey, oldtimers' hockey, charity hockey, hockey tournaments, three-on-three, contact and non-contact, floor hockey, underwater hockey, table hockey, air hockey. It can often refer also to midnight hockey or shinny, played by friends in the same arena at the same hour, year after year. Go to any arena in Canada and you'll see men in their thirties and forties, sixties and seventies even, who have played together for years or decades.

Wives and girlfriends don't come to watch you play shinny. Cell phones aren't allowed in the dressing room. Work worries are not addressed by the shinny brethren, and for that one hour a week only jokes about things like broken sticks and being tripped by the blueline are admissible. References to Churchill, Shakespeare, or Darwin are shot down with quotes from *Slapshot*, Mike Palmateer, or Harry Neale.

The shinny group also has its own slang. The game is referred to as "a skate," "an hour," or by the term "we have ice." A newcomer is a "guest" and a goalie a "target" or "'tender." Skates are "blades," pucks are "biscuits," teeth are "Chiclets," and helmets are "lids." One person is responsible for water bottles, another for pucks. One guy makes sure you have two goalies and that everyone's paid up. You ask a buddy if the skate sharpener is any good and you watch how long the Zamboni takes because every lap takes exactly one minute away from your hour. And when you come off the ice, breathing hard, tired, and sated, the dressing room is quiet as a church—until someone starts up about the broken one-piece or the slapshot that didn't reach the goal because it was so weak. You make fun and have fun, and although you're a million miles from the NHL, you're blissfully close to paradise.

There is no age restriction on playing hockey. As long as the body is willing, the Canadian mind is always ready for a skate with the boys (or girls).

ACKNOWLEDGEMENTS

THE AUTHOR would like to thank the many people who have made this book possible: publisher Rob Sanders for his faith in the proposal, editor Derek Fairbridge, and Susan Rana, Laraine Coates, and art director Peter Cocking at Greystone.

To photographers James McCrorie and Dennis Miles, without whose participation and contributions the book would be considerably the worse. As always, to everyone at the Hockey Hall of Fame for support: Craig Campbell, Phil Pritchard, Danielle Siciliano, Miragh Addis, Izak Westgate, Darren Boyko, Ron Ellis, Kevin Shea, Anthony Fusco, Steve Poirier, Tyler Wolosewich, and Mike Bolt.

Also, to the many people who gave of their time, gave images, or gave assistance in other ways, notably Carl Lavigne at the Montreal Canadiens, Matt Williams and Lynn Henry at Anansi, Brian McFarlane, Father Kennedy at St. Mike's, Saul Miller, Danny Braun, Tom Fergus, Erin Riley, Vic Hadfield, Denis Brodeur, Nancy Glowinski and David Pillinger at Reuters, Paul Michinard and Glenn Levy at Getty Images, Andrea McCaffrey in Ottawa, Mr. and Mrs. Frank Lennon, Terry McGarry at Notre Dame, Peter Jagla and family (Sandra, Konrad, Harmony), Nick LeDonne and daughter, Andrea, Paul Patskou, Wes Savoy, Michael Oesch, Grant Krisman, Art Kennedy and Thomas Giannitsopoulou, Noah Taft, Marc and Claude Juteau at classicauctions.net, iceman Jimmy MacNeil, Anne Apps, Jim and Shawn at Bill Bolton Arena, Lisa Ghione, Raj Panikkar, Chris Bolton, Chris Szarka, Serge Barbe and Serge Blondin, Erika Fisher and John Miller, Meredith Michetti, Antonietta Cole, and Lisa Stopay at Tim Hortons®, and Tom Stewart and Stompin' Tom Connors.

To my agent, Dean Cooke, and his associate Suzanne Brandreth. A special thanks also to Szymon Szemberg at the IIHF for his vital support and friendship. And lastly to my family, who endure my hours and schedule with, well, forbearance: Liz, Ian, Zachary, Emily, Mom for giving me everything I done got, and Mary Jane, whose gospel rendering of "Dem Bones" is second to none. To all a big thanks.

pp. 9, 17, 21, 22, 25, 26, 30, 46, 65, 69, 78, 81, 90, 93, 101, 102, 105, 114, 121, 122, cover—James McCrorie & Dennis Miles

pp. 10, 13—National Archives

pp. 14, 33, 34, 38, 45, 50, 61, 62, 109, cover—Hockey Hall of Fame Archives

p. 18—Montreal Canadiens Hockey Club

p. 29—Marc and Claude Juteau/ www.classicauctions.net

p. 37—Tim Hortons/The TDL Group Corp.

p. 41—Frank Lennon

p. 42—Stompin' Tom Ltd.

Photo used with permission of Stompin' Tom Ltd.

pp. 49, 82—Getty Images

p. 53—Denis Brodeur

p. 54, cover—Paul Bereswill/Hockey Hall of Fame

p. 57—House of Anansi Press

p. 58—City of Montreal Archives

p. 66—Peter H. Stranks

pp. 70, 73, 117, cover—Reuters

pp. 74, 85—*Edmonton Journal*

p. 77—Athol Murray College of Notre Dame

pp. 86, 97, 125, cover—Dave Sandford/ Hockey Hall of Fame

p. 89—City of Ottawa Archives

p. 94—Peter Jagla Collection

p. 98—Mike Bolt/Hockey Hall of Fame

p. 106—Jimmy MacNeil Collection

p. 110—Andrew Podnieks

p. 113—Office of Senator Frank Mahovlich

p. 118—Brian Smith

p. 126—Nick LeDonne Collection

p. 129—Saul Miller

p. 130—Ottawa Senators/Hockey Hall of Fame

p. 133—Erin Riley

cover—Wesley Savoy

"Tim Hortons" and "Timbits" are registered trademarks of The TDL Marks Corporation and are used under license by The TDL Group Corp.